Table of Contents

Glossary

Analogy. A way of comparing things to show how they relate. For example: nose is to smell as tongue is to taste.

Classifying. Putting similar things into categories.

Context. A way to figure out the meaning of a new word by relating it to the other words in the sentence.

Fact. Information that can be proved. Example: Hawaii is a state.

Homographs. Words that have the same spelling but different meaning and pronunciations.

Idioms. A phrase that says one thing but actually means something quite different. Example: Now that's a horse of a different color!

Inference. Using logic to figure out what is unspoken but evident.

Main Idea. Finding the most important points.

Opinion. Information that tells what someone thinks. It cannot be proved. Example: Hawaii is the prettiest state.

Prefix. A syllable at the beginning of a word that changes its meaning.

Scan. Looking for certain words in a reading selection to locate facts or answer questions.

Sequencing. Putting things in logical order.

Similes. Comparing two things that have something in common but are really very different. The words **like** and **as** are used in similes. Example: The baby was as happy as a lark.

Skim. Reading quickly to get a general idea of what a reading selection is about.

Suffix. A syllable at the end of a word that changes its meaning.

Syllable. Word divisions. Each syllable has one vowel sound.

Syllabication. Dividing words into parts, each with a vowel sound.

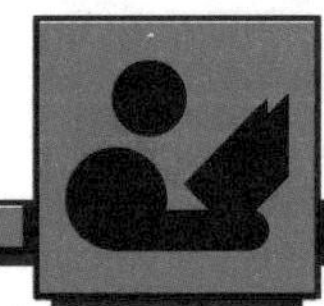

Name: ______________________

Adding Suffixes

The suffixes **-ant** and **-ent** mean a person or thing that does something. Example, one who occupies a place is the occup**ant**.

Directions: Combine each root word and suffix to make a new word. (When a word ends in silent **e**, keep the **e** before adding a suffix beginning with a consonant. Drop the **e** before adding a suffix beginning with a vowel.)

Example: announce + ment = announcement; announce + ing + announcing.) The first one is done for you.

ROOT WORD	SUFFIX	NEW WORD
observe	-ant	observant
contest	-ant	____________
please	-ant	____________
preside	-ent	____________
differ	-ent	____________

Directions: Using the meanings in the parentheses, complete each sentence with one of the words you just formed. One is done for you.

1. To be a good scientist you must be very observant. (pay careful attention)

2. Her perfume had a strong but very ____________ smell. (pleasing)

3. Because the bridge was out, we had to find a ____________ route home. (not the same)

4. The game show ____________ jumped up and down when she won the grand prize. (person who competes in a contest)

5. Next week we will elect a new student council ____________. (highest officer)

Name: ______________________

Make New Words

The suffix **-al** means of, like, or suitable for; **-ative** means having the nature of or relating to; **-ive** means have or tend to be.

Directions: Combine each root word and suffix to form a new word. Remember that the spelling of the root word sometimes changes when a suffix is added. The first one is done for you.

ROOT WORD	SUFFIX	NEW WORD
logic	-al	logical
imagine	-ative	______________
talk	-ative	______________
impress	-ive	______________
attract	-ive	______________

Directions: Using the meanings in the parentheses, complete each sentence with one of the words you just formed.

1. Because of his acting ability, Michael was the ______________ choice to have the lead part in the school play. (decided with reasoning)

2. Our history teacher is a rather ______________ man, who likes to tell jokes and stories. (fond of talking)

3. That book has such an ______________ plot! (showing imagination)

4. Monica thought the dress in the store window was very ______________. (pleasing, something that attracts)

5. The high school basketball team was ______________ in its Friday night game, beating their rivals by thirty points. (making an impression on the mind or emotions)

Name: ____________________

Changing The Meanings Of Words

The prefixes **il-**, **im-**, **in-**, and **ir-** all mean not.

Directions: Divide each word into its prefix and root word. The first one is done for you.

	PREFIX	ROOT WORD
illogical	il	logic
impatient	________	________
immature	________	________
incomplete	________	________
insincere	________	________
irresponsible	________	________
irregular	________	________

Directions: Using the meanings in the parentheses, complete each sentence with one of the words you just formed.

1. I had to turn in my assignment ________________ because I was sick last night. (not finished)

2. It was ________________ for Jimmy to give me his keys because he can't get into his house without them. (not reasonable)

3. Sue and Joel were ________________ to have a party while there parents were out of town. (lacking a sense of responsiblity)

4. I sometimes get ________________ waiting for my ride to school. (a lack of patience)

5. The boys sounded ________________ when they said they were sorry. (not honest)

6. These pants didn't cost much because they are ________________ . (not straight or even)

Name: ______________________

Homographs

Directions: Write the definition from the box for the bold word in each sentence.

pres ent	*n.*	a gift
pre sent	*v.*	to introduce or offer to view
rec ord	*n.*	written or official evidence
re cord	*v.*	to keep an account of
wind	*n.*	air in motion
wind	*v.*	to tighten the spring by turning a knob, as with a watch
wound (woond)	*n.*	an injury in which the skin is broken
wound	*v.*	past tense of wind

1. I would like to **present** our new student council president, Mindy Hall.

____

2. The store made a **record** of all my payments.

____

3. Don't forget to **wind** your alarm clock before you go to sleep.

____

4. He received a serious **wound** on his hand by playing with a knife.

____

5. The **wind** knocked over my bicycle.

____

6. I bought her a birthday **present** with my allowance.

____

Name: ______________________

What Is The Correct Meaning?

Directions: Circle the correct definition of the bold word in each sentence. One is done for you.

1. Try to **flag** down a car to get us some help!	(to signal to stop) cloth used as symbol
2. We listened to the **band** play the National Anthem.	group of musicians a binding or tie
3. He was the **sole** survivor of the plane crash.	bottom of the foot one and only
4. I am going to **pound** the nail with this hammer.	to hit hard a unit of weight
5. He lived on what little **game** he could find in the woods.	animals for hunting form of entertainment
6. We are going to **book** the midnight flight from Miami.	to reserve in advance a literary work
7. The **pitcher** looked toward first base before throwing the ball.	baseball team member container for pouring
8. My grandfather and I played a **game** of checkers last night.	animals for hunting form of entertainment
9. They raise the **flag** over City Hall every morning.	to signal to stop cloth used as symbol

Name: ______________________

Similes

Directions: Choose a word from the word box to complete each comparison. One is done for you.

tack	grass	fish	mule	ox	rail	hornet	monkey

1. as stubborn as a mule
2. as strong as an ______________
3. swims like a ______________
4. as sharp as a ______________
5. as thin as a ______________
6. as mad as a ______________
7. climbs like a ______________
8. as green as ______________

Directions: Use words of your own to complete the following similes.

1. as ______________ as a tack
2. as light as a ______________
3. ______________ like a bird
4. as ______________ as honey
5. as hungry as a ______________
6. ______________ like a snake
7. as white as ______________
8. as cold as ______________

Directions: Make up similes to finish the following sentences.

1. Our new puppy sounded ______________________________.
2. The clouds were ______________________________.
3. Our new car is ______________________________.
4. The watermelon tasted ______________________________.

Name: ______________________________

Figurative Language

Directions: Write the letter of the correct meaning for the bold words in each sentence. One is done for you.

a. refusal to see or listen	**f**. pay for
b. misbehaving, acting in a wild way	**g**. unknowing
c. made a thoughtless remark	**h**. feeling very sad
d. lost an opportunity	**i**. get married
e. got angry	**j**. excited and happy

__f__ 1. My parents will **foot the bill** for my birthday party.

______ 2. Tony and Lisa will finally **tie the knot** in June.

______ 3. Sam was **down in the dumps** after he wrecked his bicycle.

______4. Sarah **put her foot in her mouth** when she was talking to our teacher.

______5. I really **missed the boat** when I turned down the chance to work after school.

______6. I got the **brush off** from Susan when I tried to ask her where she was last night.

______7. Mickey is **in the dark** about our plans to throw a surprise birthday party for him.

______8. The children were **bouncing off the walls** when the babysitter was trying to put them to bed.

______9. The students were **flying high** on the last day of school.

______10. My sister **lost her cool** when she found out that I spilled chocolate milk on her new sweater.

Name: ____________________

Review

Directions: Circle the word or phrase that best defines the bold words in each sentence.

1. The woman had a very **pleasant** voice.
   loud
   one that pleases
   strange

2. The **central** regions of the country suffer most from the drought.
   hottest
   southern
   of or near the center

3. He had a very **imaginative** excuse for not turning in his homework.
   relating to the imagination
   difficult to believe
   acceptable

4. I didn't get credit for my answer on the test because it was **incomplete**.
   not correct
   too short
   not finished

5. Will you **wind** the music box for the baby?
   air in motion
   an injury in which the skin is broken
   to tighten the spring by turning a knob

6. To enroll in the school, you must bring your birth certificate or some other legal **record** for identification.
   to keep an account
   a flat disk that plays music
   written or official evidence

7. We use the crystal **pitcher** when we have company.
   a printed likeness of a person or object
   a baseball team member
   a container for pouring

8. This block is **as light as a feather!**
   very heavy
   not heavy at all
   can be put in a cage

9. The whole family was there when Bill and Lynn **tied the knot** last weekend.
   were caught in a trap
   bought a house
   got married

10. I will have to **foot the bill** for the damage you caused.
    kick
    pay for
    seek payment

11. Carol **lost her cool** when the party was called off.
    got angry
    had a fever
    went home

12. The kite **soared like an eagle**.
    flapped and fluttered
    glided along high in the air
    crashed to the ground

Name: ______________________

Find The Words

Directions: Find each of the words from the word box in the puzzle. Some words go across, some go up and down, one is on the diagonal, and two are backwards. One is done for you.

l	c	o	n	t	i	n	e	n	t	l
o	b	e	l	a	t	i	t	u	d	e
n	o	c	e	x	h	e	r	e	r	g
g	h	e	m	i	s	p	h	e	r	e
i	e	t	o	s	o	o	e	q	o	n
t	a	o	c	l	m	l	m	u	t	d
u	n	r	e	b	o	l	g	a	e	l
d	n	e	a	i	s	e	v	t	l	r
e	s	t	n	u	v	e	h	o	a	x
c	o	m	p	a	s	s	e	r	c	m
s	i	x	o	c	a	n	t	o	s	e

axis	compass
equator	globe
latitude	longitude
legend	ocean
pole	
hemisphere	
continent	
scale	

Directions: Each sentence tells something about maps but the bold words are jumbled up. Rearrange the letters to spell words from the word box.

1. East and west distances are measured in **gudelnoti**. ______________
2. Half of the earth is called a **premsheehi**. ______________
3. The **quotare** is an imaginary line that divides the earth's surface into the Northern and Southern Hemispheres. ______________
4. Distances north and south of the equator are measured in **iduttale**. ______________
5. The **blego** is the most complete and accurate map of the earth. ______________
6. The **sixa** is an imaginary line on which the earth turns. ______________
7. The seven largest land forms, including Africa, Australia, and North America, are called **cennitonts**. ______________
8. The four largest bodies of water, including the Pacific and the Atlantic, are the **canoes**. ______________

Name: ______________________

The Continents

Directions: Read the facts about the seven continents and follow the directions.

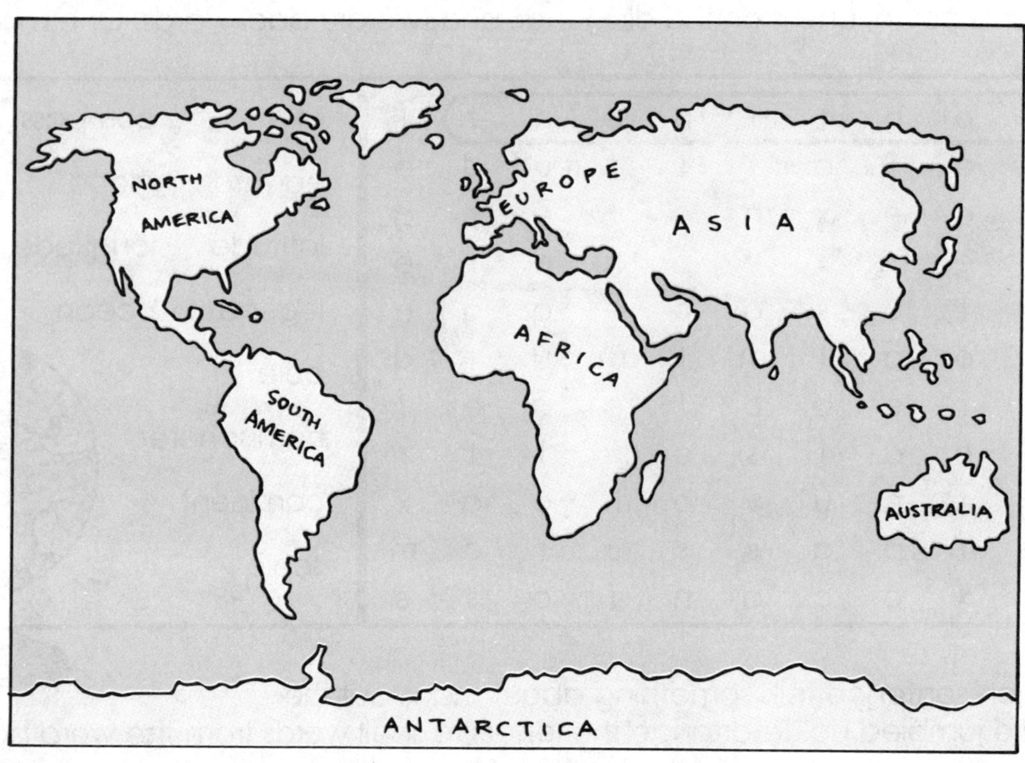

1. **Asia** is the biggest continent. It has the largest land mass and the largest population. Draw a star on Asia.
2. **Africa** is the second largest continent. Put a 2 on Africa.
3. **Australia** is the smallest continent in area: 3 million square miles compared to 17 million square miles for Asia. Write 3,000,000 on Australia.
4. **Australia** is not a very crowded continent. But it does not rank lowest in population. That honor goes to **Antarctica**, which has no permanent population at all! This ice-covered continent is too cold for life. Write ZERO on Antarctica.
5. **Australia** and **Antarctica** are the only continents entirely separated by water. Draw circles around Australia and Antarctica.
6. **North America** and **South America** are joined together by a narrow strip of land. It is called **Central America**. Write an **N** on North America, an **S** on South America, and a **C** on Central America.
7. **Asia** and **Europe** are joined together over such a great distance that they are sometimes called just one continent. The name given it is Eurasia. Draw lines under the names of the two continents in "Eurasia."

Name: ______________________________

Winter Sleep

In many areas of the world winter weather is very harsh on living things. Plants and animals must find ways to survive the cold temperatures and lack of food and water. Plants and trees drop their leaves and rest. Many birds, some insects, and a few other animals migrate during the winter. Some animals hibernate. Hibernation is sometimes known as "winter sleep."

Mammals that hibernate include woodchucks (which are also called groundhogs), skunks, and some kinds of squirrels, bats, and, of course, bears. To prepare for the winter months, these animals store up fat on their bodies during the summer and fall. They may hide food or take it into their dens or burrows. Some animals line their winter "homes" with grass or hay.

When the temperatures drop, they crawl into their dens. The close space helps to hold in the heat of their bodies. They fall into a deep sleep in which their bodies become almost lifeless. A hibernating bear may rouse itself occasionally and even wander about looking for a new resting place before settling into another deep sleep. The animals use up the stored fat little by little. When they awaken in the spring with the warmer weather, they are thin — and ready for a big meal.

Directions: Number in order the steps a hibernating animal goes through to escape the cold winter weather.

____ They fall into a deep sleep in which their bodies become almost lifeless.

____ These animals store up fat on their bodies during the summer and fall.

____ When the temperatures drop, they crawl into their dens. The close space helps to hold in the heat of their bodies.

____ When they awaken in the spring with the warmer weather, they are thin — and ready for a big meal.

____ The animals use up the stored fat little by little.

____ Some animals hide food or take it into their dens or burrows. They may line their winter "homes" with grass or hay.

Name: ____________________

Make A Bird Feeder

Bird watching can be fun and educational. By providing for their basic needs — food, water, shelter, and a place to nest — you can attract birds to your own yard, no matter where you live. The easiest way to attract birds is to build a feeder and stock it with food. Here are step-by-step instructions for making a simple one.

The materials you will need are a large tin can (a two-pound coffee can is a good size), a wire coat hanger, a cork, one six-inch aluminum-foil pie pan, and a nine-inch foil pan.

First, using the kind of can opener that cuts small triangles, make five holes in the side of the can right above the bottom rim. Next, straighten the coat hanger and bend one end into a loop. Poke holes the size of the wire in the middle of the two foil pans. Cut another hole in the center of the bottom of the can. Try to make all of the holes in the exact center so they will line up.

With the smaller pan right side up, push the straight end of the wire through its hole and then through the hole in the can. Turn the larger pan upside down and put the wire through its hole. Fill the can with mixed birdseed, making sure that the seed falls through the holes onto the bottom pan. Then force the cork down the wire until it rests tightly against the top pan. Finally, make a hook in the top of the wire to use as a hanger. Hang your feeder where you can easily see it. Sit back and watch for the birds to come!

Directions: Number in order the steps to building the bird feeder.

____ Cuts holes the size of the wire in the middle of the foil pans and the can.

____ Fill the can with birdseed and make sure it falls through the holes in the sides of the can onto the bottom pan.

____ With a can opener, make five openings in the side of the can near the bottom rim.

____ Form a hook in the end of the wire to use as a hanger.

____ Gather together a large tin can, two foil pans, a wire coat hanger, and a cork.

____ Straighten the coat hanger and make a loop in one end.

____ With the smaller pan turned right side up, push the wire through the holes in the pan and the tin can.

____ Hang up your bird feeder and watch for the birds to come!

____ Turn the larger pan upside down and push the wire through the hole.

____ Force the cork down the wire until it fits tightly against the top plate.

Name: ______________________

Feed The Birds

Can you imagine feeding birds right from your hand? Here is how you can do just that!

Begin by attracting birds to your windowsill with a bird feeder (such as the one described on page 14). Once they are used to feeding there, you are ready to move to the next part of the plan.

Get a piece of wood that is about two or three feet long and a couple inches wide. Put this "arm" in the sleeve of an old coat or shirt and attach an old glove to the bottom with a thumbtack. Now put the "arm" out of the window over the bird feeder, and close the window to hold it in place. Put some birdseed on the glove every day for a week or so until the birds get used to eating from it.

Next put your own arm and hand inside the sleeve and glove. Rest your arm on the windowsill so it won't get tired and hold some birdseed in your hand. Be very still! After a few days, the birds will get used to eating from your gloved hand. The next step is to take off the glove and put the seed in your bare hand. You will have birds feeding out of your hand in no time!

Directions: Number in order the steps for getting birds to eat from your hand.

____ Rest your arm on the windowsill and put birdseed in your gloved hand. Hold very still!

____ Make an "arm" from a piece of wood. Put it inside the sleeve of a coat or shirt and attach an old glove to the bottom.

____ When the birds become used to eating from your gloved hand, take off the glove.

____ Stick the "arm" out of the window over the bird feeder and put birdseed in the glove.

____ Put birdseed in your bare hand and wait for the birds to begin eating right from your hand!

____ Start attracting birds to your windowsill with a bird feeder. Let them get used to feeding there.

____ Once the birds are used to feeding from the "arm" you made, put your own hand and arm into the sleeve and glove.

Name: ____________________

Review

For a long time, people believed that the caterpillar and the butterfly were two unrelated insects. Today, however, we know that they are the same creature at different stages of its development.

This remarkable life cycle begins when the female butterfly lays her eggs — which can number in the hundreds — on a plant that will provide just the right food for the caterpillars that will hatch. The caterpillar begins eating right away and continues to eat constantly. Soon it is too big for its skin. The skin splits to allow the caterpillar to crawl out. This is called molting. The caterpillar may molt as many as ten times before beginning the next stage of development.

During the next stage, called the pupa, there seems to be little activity. In fact, many changes are taking place inside the caterpillar. The caterpillar finds a place, usually on a twig, and deposits a sticky liquid to form a pad. The caterpillar then hangs upside down. The skin molts one final time, leaving the pupa. Immediately, a hard shell called a chrysalis or cocoon is formed.

After 10 to 14 days, the cocoon suddenly bursts open. A few seconds later, the butterfly has come out. At first its wings are pressed together. Fluid is pumped through hollow veins until the wings are fully expanded. The butterfly spreads its wings to dry and harden. Then the fluid is withdrawn from the wing veins. The butterfly is now ready to fly.

Directions: Number in order the stages of a butterfly's life cycle.

____ A few seconds later, the butterfly has come out.

____ A hard shell called a chrysalis or cocoon is formed.

____ The female butterfly lays her eggs on a plant.

____ The caterpillar's skin splits to allow it to crawl out.

____ The caterpillar eats constantly.

____ The butterfly is now ready to fly.

____ After 10 to 14 days, the cocoon suddenly bursts open.

____ The caterpillar's skin molts one final time, leaving the pupa.

____ Fluid expands the butterfly's wings, which then dry and harden.

ANSWER KEY

This Answer Key has been designed so that it may be easily removed if you so desire.

GRADE 5 READING

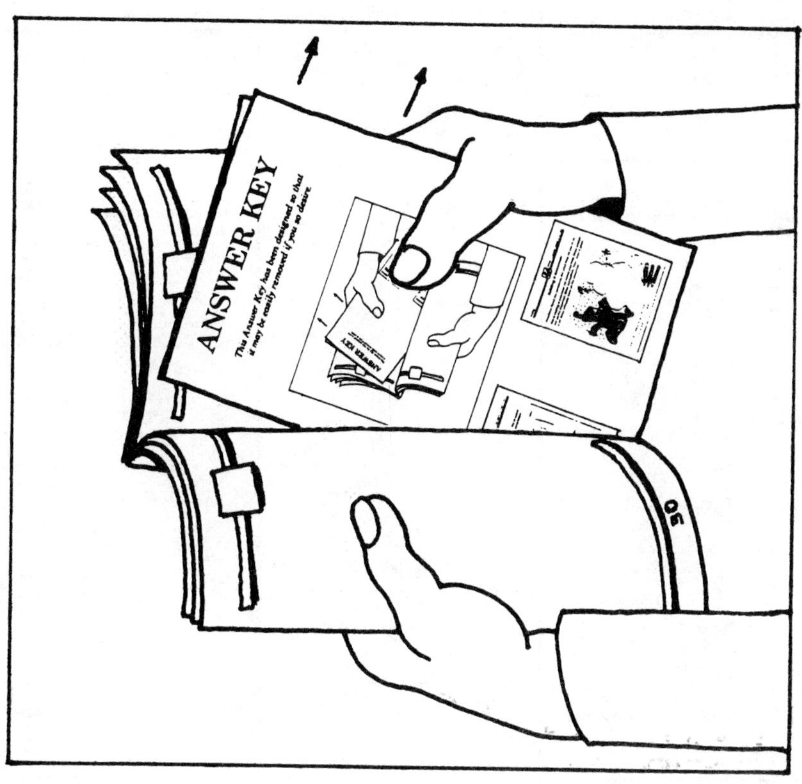

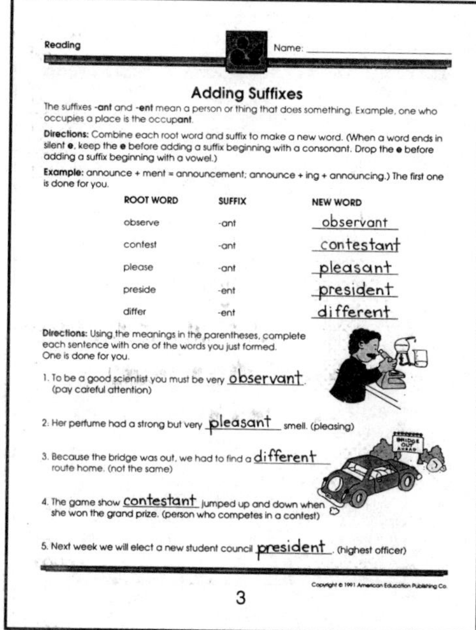

Reading — Name: ____________

Adding Suffixes

The suffixes **-ant** and **-ent** mean a person or thing that does something. Example, one who occupies a place is the occup**ant**.

Directions: Combine each root word and suffix to make a new word. (When a word ends in silent **e**, keep the **e** before adding a suffix beginning with a consonant. Drop the **e** before adding a suffix beginning with a vowel.)

Example: announce + ment = announcement; announce + ing + announcing.) The first one is done for you.

ROOT WORD	SUFFIX	NEW WORD
observe	-ant	observant
contest	-ant	contestant
please	-ant	pleasant
preside	-ent	president
differ	-ent	different

Directions: Using the meanings in the parentheses, complete each sentence with one of the words you just formed. One is done for you.

1. To be a good scientist you must be very observant. (pay careful attention)
2. Her perfume had a strong but very pleasant smell. (pleasing)
3. Because the bridge was out, we had to find a different route home. (not the same)
4. The game show contestant jumped up and down when she won the grand prize. (person who competes in a contest)
5. Next week we will elect a new student council president. (highest officer)

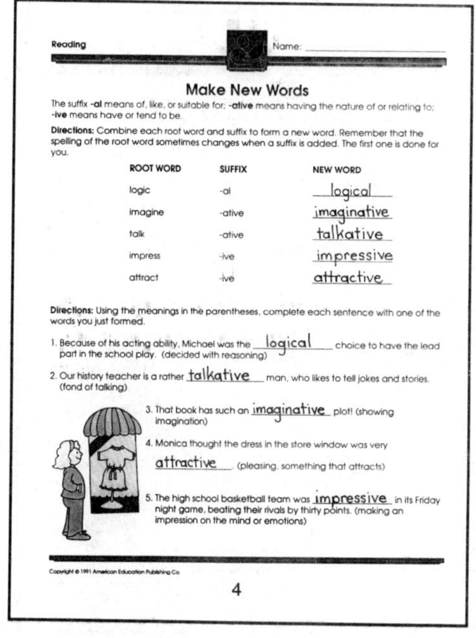

Reading — Name: ____________

Make New Words

The suffix **-al** means of, like, or suitable for; **-ative** means having the nature of or relating to; **-ive** means have or tend to be.

Directions: Combine each root word and suffix to form a new word. Remember that the spelling of the root word sometimes changes when a suffix is added. The first one is done for you.

ROOT WORD	SUFFIX	NEW WORD
logic	-al	logical
imagine	-ative	imaginative
talk	-ative	talkative
impress	-ive	impressive
attract	-ive	attractive

Directions: Using the meanings in the parentheses, complete each sentence with one of the words you just formed.

1. Because of his acting ability, Michael was the logical choice to have the lead part in the school play. (decided with reasoning)
2. Our history teacher is a rather talkative man, who likes to tell jokes and stories. (fond of talking)
3. That book has such an imaginative plot! (showing imagination)
4. Monica thought the dress in the store window was very attractive. (pleasing, something that attracts)
5. The high school basketball team was impressive in its Friday night game, beating their rivals by thirty points. (making an impression on the mind or emotions)

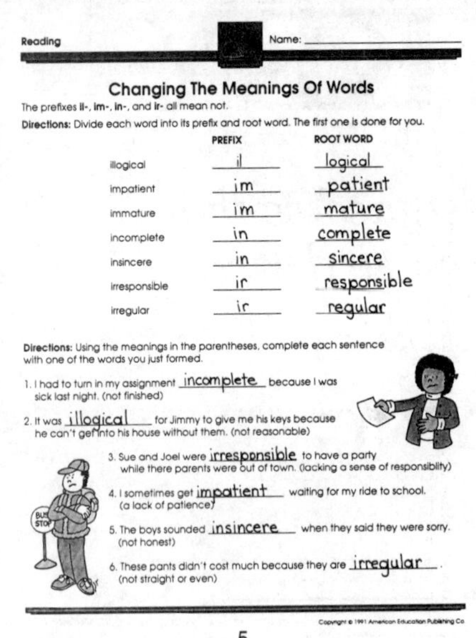
Reading Name: ____________

Changing The Meanings Of Words

The prefixes **il-**, **im-**, **in-**, and **ir-** all mean not.

Directions: Divide each word into its prefix and root word. The first one is done for you.

	PREFIX	ROOT WORD
illogical	il	logical
impatient	im	patient
immature	im	mature
incomplete	in	complete
insincere	in	sincere
irresponsible	ir	responsible
irregular	ir	regular

Directions: Using the meanings in the parentheses, complete each sentence with one of the words you just formed.

1. I had to turn in my assignment incomplete because I was sick last night. (not finished)
2. It was illogical for Jimmy to give me his keys because he can't get into his house without them. (not reasonable)
3. Sue and Joel were irresponsible to have a party while there parents were out of town. (lacking a sense of responsibility)
4. I sometimes get impatient waiting for my ride to school. (a lack of patience)
5. The boys sounded insincere when they said they were sorry. (not honest)
6. These pants didn't cost much because they are irregular. (not straight or even)

Copyright © 1991 American Education Publishing Co.

5

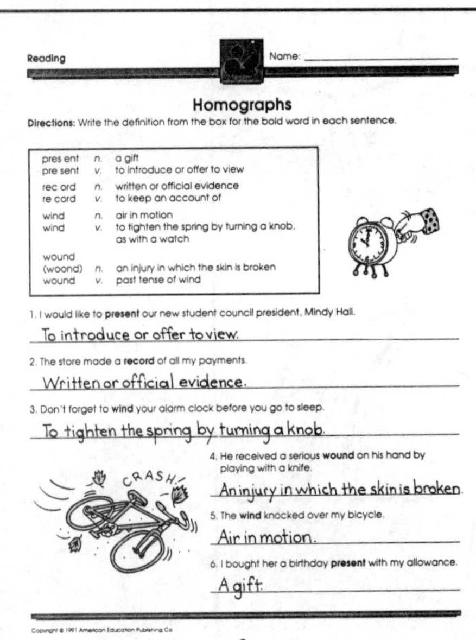
Reading Name: ____________

Homographs

Directions: Write the definition from the box for the bold word in each sentence.

pres ent	n.	a gift
pre sent	v.	to introduce or offer to view
rec ord	n.	written or official evidence
re cord	v.	to keep an account of
wind	n.	air in motion
wind	v.	to tighten the spring by turning a knob, as with a watch
wound (woond)	n.	an injury in which the skin is broken
wound	v.	past tense of wind

1. I would like to **present** our new student council president, Mindy Hall.
   To introduce or offer to view.
2. The store made a **record** of all my payments.
   Written or official evidence.
3. Don't forget to **wind** your alarm clock before you go to sleep.
   To tighten the spring by turning a knob.
4. He received a serious **wound** on his hand by playing with a knife.
   An injury in which the skin is broken.
5. The **wind** knocked over my bicycle.
   Air in motion.
6. I bought her a birthday **present** with my allowance.
   A gift.

Copyright © 1991 American Education Publishing Co.

6

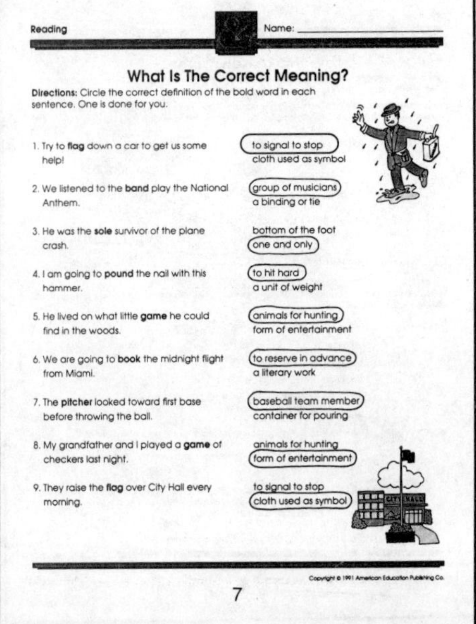
Reading Name: ____________

What Is The Correct Meaning?

Directions: Circle the correct definition of the bold word in each sentence. One is done for you.

1. Try to **flag** down a car to get us some help! — (to signal to stop) / cloth used as symbol
2. We listened to the **band** play the National Anthem. — (group of musicians) / a binding or tie
3. He was the **sole** survivor of the plane crash. — bottom of the foot / (one and only)
4. I am going to **pound** the nail with this hammer. — (to hit hard) / a unit of weight
5. He lived on what little **game** he could find in the woods. — (animals for hunting) / form of entertainment
6. We are going to **book** the midnight flight from Miami. — (to reserve in advance) / a literary work
7. The **pitcher** looked toward first base before throwing the ball. — (baseball team member) / container for pouring
8. My grandfather and I played a **game** of checkers last night. — animals for hunting / (form of entertainment)
9. They raise the **flag** over City Hall every morning. — to signal to stop / (cloth used as symbol)

Copyright © 1991 American Education Publishing Co.

7

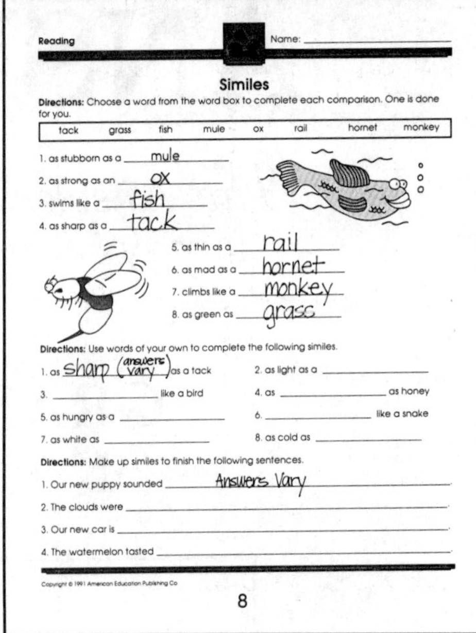
Reading Name: ____________

Similes

Directions: Choose a word from the word box to complete each comparison. One is done for you.

tack	grass	fish	mule	ox	rail	hornet	monkey

1. as stubborn as a mule
2. as strong as an ox
3. swims like a fish
4. as sharp as a tack
5. as thin as a rail
6. as mad as a hornet
7. climbs like a monkey
8. as green as grasс

Directions: Use words of your own to complete the following similes.

1. as sharp (answers vary) as a tack
2. as light as a ____
3. ____ like a bird
4. as ____ as honey
5. as hungry as a ____
6. ____ like a snake
7. as white as ____
8. as cold as ____

Directions: Make up similes to finish the following sentences.

1. Our new puppy sounded Answers Vary
2. The clouds were ____
3. Our new car is ____
4. The watermelon tasted ____

Copyright © 1991 American Education Publishing Co.

8

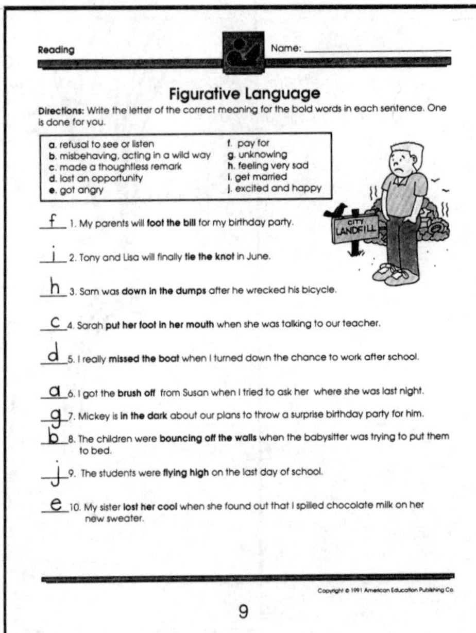
Reading Name: ____________

Figurative Language

Directions: Write the letter of the correct meaning for the bold words in each sentence. One is done for you.

a. refusal to see or listen	f. pay for
b. misbehaving, acting in a wild way	g. unknowing
c. made a thoughtless remark	h. feeling very sad
d. lost an opportunity	i. get married
e. got angry	j. excited and happy

f 1. My parents will **foot the bill** for my birthday party.
i 2. Tony and Lisa will finally **tie the knot** in June.
h 3. Sam was **down in the dumps** after he wrecked his bicycle.
c 4. Sarah **put her foot in her mouth** when she was talking to our teacher.
d 5. I really **missed the boat** when I turned down the chance to work after school.
a 6. I got the **brush off** from Susan when I tried to ask her where she was last night.
g 7. Mickey is **in the dark** about our plans to throw a surprise birthday party for him.
b 8. The children were **bouncing off the walls** when the babysitter was trying to put them to bed.
j 9. The students were **flying high** on the last day of school.
e 10. My sister **lost her cool** when she found out that I spilled chocolate milk on her new sweater.

Copyright © 1991 American Education Publishing Co.

9

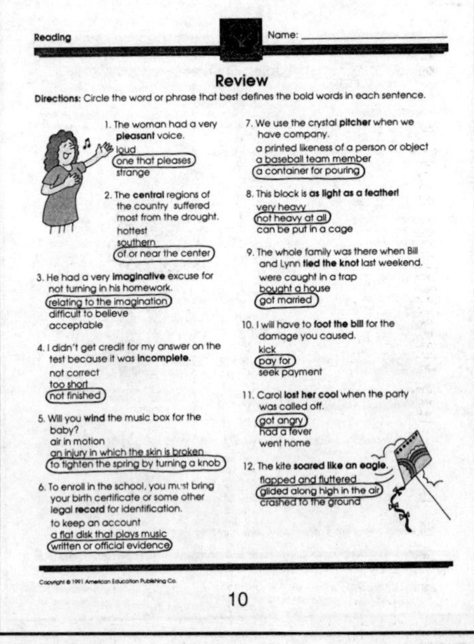
Reading Name: ____________

Review

Directions: Circle the word or phrase that best defines the bold words in each sentence.

1. The woman had a very **pleasant** voice.
   loud / (one that pleases) / strange
2. The **central** regions of the country suffered most from the drought.
   hottest / southern / (of or near the center)
3. He had a very **imaginative** excuse for not turning in his homework.
   (relating to the imagination) / difficult to believe / acceptable
4. I didn't get credit for my answer on the test because it was **incomplete**.
   not correct / too short / (not finished)
5. Will you **wind** the music box for the baby?
   air in motion / an injury in which the skin is broken / (to tighten the spring by turning a knob)
6. To enroll in the school, you must bring your birth certificate or some other legal **record** for identification.
   to keep an account / a flat disk that plays music / (written or official evidence)
7. We use the crystal **pitcher** when we have company.
   a printed likeness of a person or object / a baseball team member / (a container for pouring)
8. This block is **as light as a feather!**
   very heavy / (not heavy at all) / can be put in a cage
9. The whole family was there when Bill and Lynn **tied the knot** last weekend.
   were caught in a trap / bought a house / (got married)
10. I will have to **foot the bill** for the damage you caused.
    kick / (pay for) / seek payment
11. Carol **lost her cool** when the party was called off.
    (got angry) / had a fever / went home
12. The kite **soared like an eagle.**
    flapped and fluttered / (glided along high in the air) / crashed to the ground

Copyright © 1991 American Education Publishing Co.

10

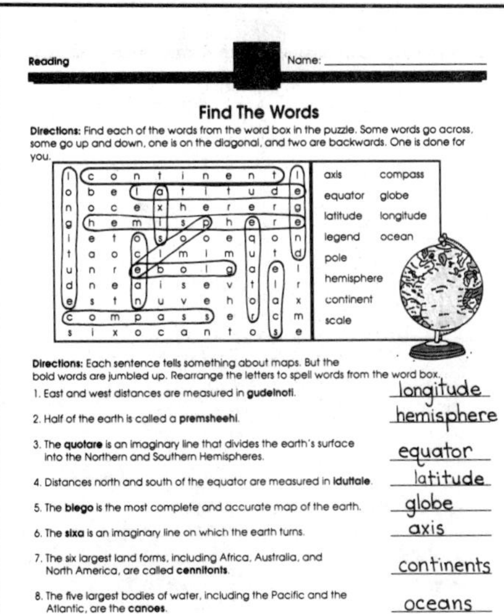

Find The Words

Directions: Find each of the words from the word box in the puzzle. Some words go across, some go up and down, one is on the diagonal, and two are backwards. One is done for you.

l	c	o	n	t	i	n	e	n	t	l	
o	b	e	l	a	t	i	t	u	d	e	
n	o	c	e	x	h	e	r	e	r	g	
g	h	e	m	i	s	p	h	e	r	e	
i	e	t	o	s	o	o	e	q	o	n	
t	a	o	c	l	m	i	m	u	t	d	
u	n	r	e	b	o	l	g	a	e	l	
d	n	e	a	i	s	e	v	t	l	r	
e	s	t	n	u	v	e	h	o	a	x	
c	o	m	p	a	s	s	e	r	c	m	
s	i	x	o	c	a	n	t	o	s	e	

axis	compass
equator	globe
latitude	longitude
legend	ocean
pole	
hemisphere	
continent	
scale	

Directions: Each sentence tells something about maps. But the bold words are jumbled up. Rearrange the letters to spell words from the word box.

1. East and west distances are measured in **gudelnoti**. longitude
2. Half of the earth is called a **premsheehl**. hemisphere
3. The **quotare** is an imaginary line that divides the earth's surface into the Northern and Southern Hemispheres. equator
4. Distances north and south of the equator are measured in **iduttale**. latitude
5. The **blego** is the most complete and accurate map of the earth. globe
6. The **sixa** is an imaginary line on which the earth turns. axis
7. The six largest land forms, including Africa, Australia, and North America, are called **cennitonts**. continents
8. The five largest bodies of water, including the Pacific and the Atlantic, are the **canoes**. oceans

The Continents

Directions: Read the facts about the seven continents and follow the directions.

1. **Asia** is the biggest continent. It has the largest land mass and the largest population. Draw a star on Asia.
2. **Africa** is the second largest continent. Put a 2 on Africa.
3. **Australia** is the smallest continent in area: 3 million square miles compared to 17 million square miles for Asia. Write 3,000,000 on Australia.
4. **Australia** is not a very crowded continent. But it does not rank lowest in population. That honor goes to **Antarctica**, which has no permanent population at all! This ice-covered continent is too cold for life. Write ZERO on Antarctica.
5. **Australia** and **Antarctica** are the only continents entirely separated by water. Draw circles around Australia and Antarctica.
6. **North America** and **South America** are joined together by a narrow strip of land. It is called **Central America**. Write an **N** on North America, an **S** on South America, and a **C** on Central America.
7. **Asia** and **Europe** are joined together over such a great distance that they are sometimes called just one continent. The name given it is Eurasia. Draw lines under the names of the two continents in "Eurasia."

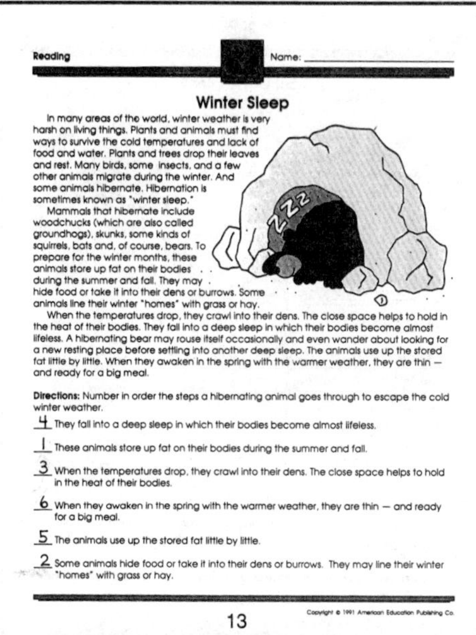

Winter Sleep

In many areas of the world, winter weather is very harsh on living things. Plants and animals must find ways to survive the cold temperatures and lack of food and water. Plants and trees drop their leaves and rest. Many birds, some insects, and a few other animals migrate during the winter. And some animals hibernate. Hibernation is sometimes known as "winter sleep."

Mammals that hibernate include woodchucks (which are also called groundhogs), skunks, some kinds of squirrels, bats and, of course, bears. To prepare for the winter months, these animals store up fat on their bodies during the summer and fall. They may hide food or take it into their dens or burrows. Some animals line their winter "homes" with grass or hay.

When the temperatures drop, they crawl into their dens. The close space helps to hold in the heat of their bodies. They fall into a deep sleep in which their bodies become almost lifeless. A hibernating bear may rouse itself occasionally and even wander about looking for a new resting place before settling into another deep sleep. The animals use up the stored fat little by little. When they awaken in the spring with the warmer weather, they are thin — and ready for a big meal.

Directions: Number in order the steps a hibernating animal goes through to escape the cold winter weather.

4 They fall into a deep sleep in which their bodies become almost lifeless.

1 These animals store up fat on their bodies during the summer and fall.

3 When the temperatures drop, they crawl into their dens. The close space helps to hold in the heat of their bodies.

6 When they awaken in the spring with the warmer weather, they are thin — and ready for a big meal.

5 The animals use up the stored fat little by little.

2 Some animals hide food or take it into their dens or burrows. They may line their winter "homes" with grass or hay.

Make A Bird Feeder

Bird-watching can be fun and educational. By providing for their basic needs — food, water, shelter, and a place to nest — you can attract birds to your own yard, no matter where you live. The easiest way to attract birds is to build a feeder and stock it with food. Here are step-by-step instructions for making a simple one.

The materials you will need are a large tin can (a two-pound coffee can is a good size), a wire coat hanger, a cork, one six-inch aluminum-foil pie pan, and a nine-inch foil pan.

First, using the kind of can opener that cuts small triangles, make five holes in the side of the can right above the bottom rim. Next, straighten the coat hanger and bend one end into a loop. Poke holes the size of the wire in the middle of the two foil pans. Cut another hole in the center of the bottom of the can. Try to make all of the holes in the exact center so they will line up.

With the smaller pan right side up, push the straight end of the wire through its hole and then through the hole in the can. Turn the larger pan upside down and put the wire through its hole. Fill the can with mixed birdseed, making sure that the seed falls through the holes onto the bottom pan. Then force the cork down the wire until it rests tightly against the top pan. Finally, make a hook in the top of the wire to use as a hanger. Hang your feeder where you can easily see it. Sit back and watch for the birds to come!

Directions: Number in order the steps to building the bird feeder.

4 Cuts holes the size of the wire in the middle of the foil pans and the can.

7 Fill the can with birdseed and make sure it falls through the holes in the sides of the can onto the bottom pan.

2 With a can opener, make five openings in the side of the can near the bottom rim.

9 Form a hook in the end of the wire to use as a hanger.

1 Gather together a large tin can, two foil pans, a wire coat hanger, and a cork.

3 Straighten the coat hanger and make a loop in one end.

5 With the smaller pan turned right side up, push the wire through the holes in the pan and the tin can.

10 Hang up your bird feeder and watch for the birds to come!

6 Turn the larger pan upside down and push the wire through the hole.

8 Force the cork down the wire until it fits tightly against the top plate.

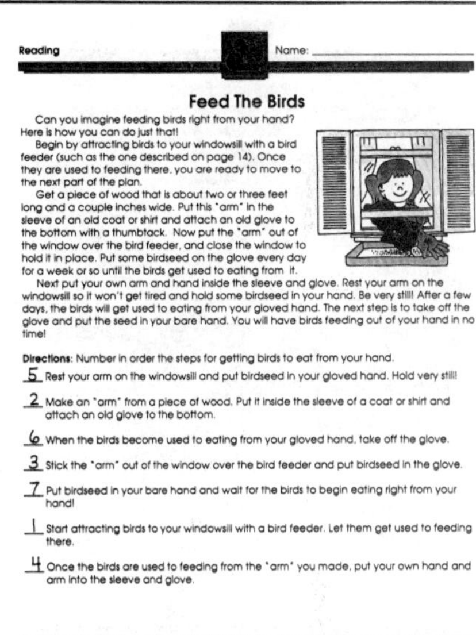

Feed The Birds

Can you imagine feeding birds right from your hand? Here is how you can do just that!

Begin by attracting birds to your windowsill with a bird feeder (such as the one described on page 14). Once they are used to feeding there, you are ready to move to the next part of the plan.

Get a piece of wood that is about two or three feet long and a couple inches wide. Put this "arm" in the sleeve of an old coat or shirt and attach an old glove to the bottom with a thumbtack. Now put the "arm" out of the window over the bird feeder, and close the window to hold it in place. Put some birdseed on the glove every day for a week or so until the birds get used to eating from it.

Next put your own arm and hand inside the sleeve and glove. Rest your arm on the windowsill so it won't get tired and hold some birdseed in your hand. Be very still! After a few days, the birds will get used to eating from your gloved hand. The next step is to take off the glove and put the seed in your bare hand. You will have birds feeding out of your hand in no time!

Directions: Number in order the steps for getting birds to eat from your hand.

5 Rest your arm on the windowsill and put birdseed in your gloved hand. Hold very still!

2 Make an "arm" from a piece of wood. Put it inside the sleeve of a coat or shirt and attach an old glove to the bottom.

6 When the birds become used to eating from your gloved hand, take off the glove.

3 Stick the "arm" out of the window over the bird feeder and put birdseed in the glove.

7 Put birdseed in your bare hand and wait for the birds to begin eating right from your hand!

1 Start attracting birds to your windowsill with a bird feeder. Let them get used to feeding there.

4 Once the birds are used to feeding from the "arm" you made, put your own hand and arm into the sleeve and glove.

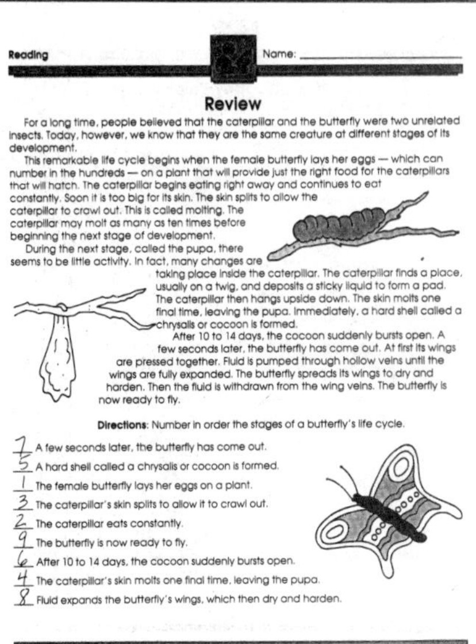

Review

For a long time, people believed that the caterpillar and the butterfly were two unrelated insects. Today, however, we know that they are the same creature at different stages of its development.

This remarkable life cycle begins when the female butterfly lays her eggs — which can number in the hundreds — on a plant that will provide just the right food for the caterpillars that will hatch. The caterpillar begins eating right away and continues to eat constantly. Soon it is too big for its skin. The skin splits to allow the caterpillar to crawl out. This is called molting. The caterpillar may molt as many as ten times before beginning the next stage of development.

During the next stage, called the pupa, there seems to be little activity. In fact, many changes are taking place inside the caterpillar. The caterpillar finds a place, usually on a twig, and deposits a sticky liquid to form a pad. The caterpillar then hangs upside down. The skin molts one final time, leaving the pupa. Immediately, a hard shell called a chrysalis or cocoon is formed.

After 10 to 14 days, the cocoon suddenly bursts open. A few seconds later, the butterfly has come out. At first its wings are pressed together. Fluid is pumped through hollow veins until the wings are fully expanded. The butterfly spreads its wings to dry and harden. Then the fluid is withdrawn from the wing veins. The butterfly is now ready to fly.

Directions: Number in order the stages of a butterfly's life cycle.

7 A few seconds later, the butterfly has come out.
5 A hard shell called a chrysalis or cocoon is formed.
1 The female butterfly lays her eggs on a plant.
3 The caterpillar's skin splits to allow it to crawl out.
2 The caterpillar eats constantly.
9 The butterfly is now ready to fly.
6 After 10 to 14 days, the cocoon suddenly bursts open.
4 The caterpillar's skin molts one final time, leaving the pupa.
8 Fluid expands the butterfly's wings, which then dry and harden.

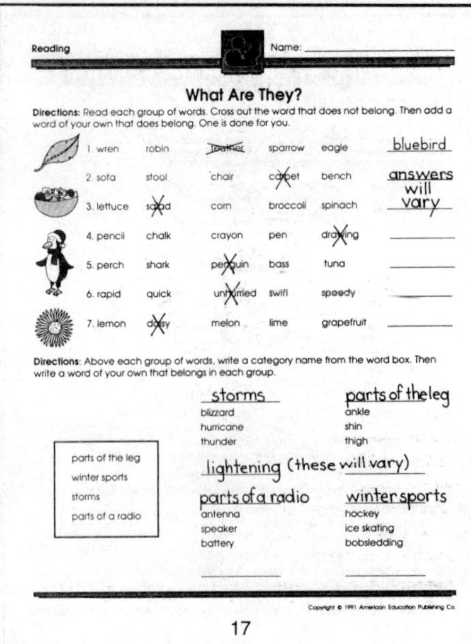
Reading Name:

What Are They?

Directions: Read each group of words. Cross out the word that does not belong. Then add a word of your own that does belong. One is done for you.

1. wren robin ~~feather~~ sparrow eagle bluebird
2. sofa stool chair ~~carpet~~ bench answers will vary
3. lettuce ~~salad~~ corn broccoli spinach
4. pencil chalk crayon pen ~~drawing~~
5. perch shark ~~penguin~~ bass tuna
6. rapid quick ~~unhurried~~ swift speedy
7. lemon ~~daisy~~ melon lime grapefruit

Directions: Above each group of words, write a category name from the word box. Then write a word of your own that belongs in each group.

parts of the leg
winter sports
storms
parts of a radio

storms: blizzard, hurricane, thunder, lightening (these will vary)

parts of the leg: ankle, shin, thigh

parts of a radio: antenna, speaker, battery

winter sports: hockey, ice skating, bobsledding

Copyright © 1991 American Education Publishing Co.

17

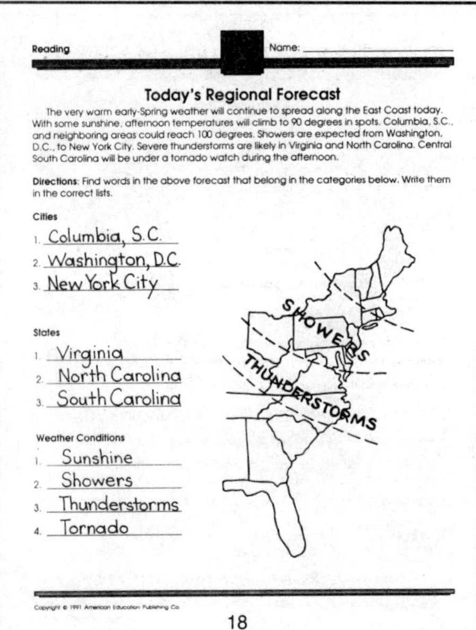
Reading Name:

Today's Regional Forecast

The very warm early-Spring weather will continue to spread along the East Coast today. With some sunshine, afternoon temperatures will climb to 90 degrees in spots. Columbia, S.C., and neighboring areas could reach 100 degrees. Showers are expected from Washington, D.C., to New York City. Severe thunderstorms are likely in Virginia and North Carolina. Central South Carolina will be under a tornado watch during the afternoon.

Directions: Find words in the above forecast that belong in the categories below. Write them in the correct lists.

Cities
1. Columbia, S.C.
2. Washington, D.C.
3. New York City

States
1. Virginia
2. North Carolina
3. South Carolina

Weather Conditions
1. Sunshine
2. Showers
3. Thunderstorms
4. Tornado

Copyright © 1991 American Education Publishing Co.

18

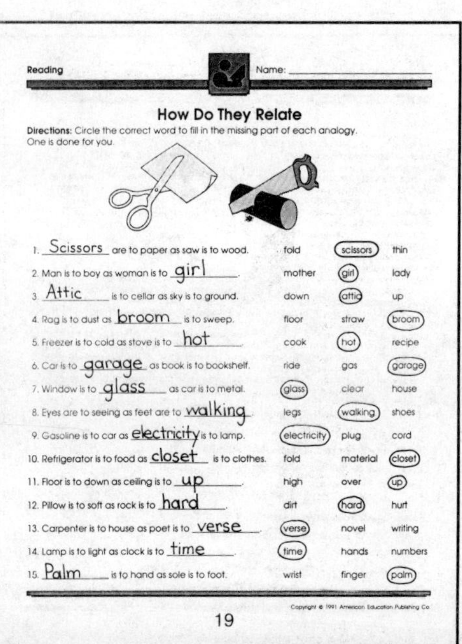
Reading Name:

How Do They Relate

Directions: Circle the correct word to fill in the missing part of each analogy. One is done for you.

1. Scissors are to paper as saw is to wood. — fold (scissors) thin
2. Man is to boy as woman is to girl. — mother (girl) lady
3. Attic is to cellar as sky is to ground. — down (attic) up
4. Rag is to dust as broom is to sweep. — floor straw (broom)
5. Freezer is to cold as stove is to hot. — cook (hot) recipe
6. Car is to garage as book is to bookshelf. — ride gas (garage)
7. Window is to glass as car is to metal. — (glass) clear house
8. Eyes are to seeing as feet are to walking. — legs (walking) shoes
9. Gasoline is to car as electricity is to lamp. — (electricity) plug cord
10. Refrigerator is to food as closet is to clothes. — fold material (closet)
11. Floor is to down as ceiling is to up. — high over (up)
12. Pillow is to soft as rock is to hard. — dirt (hard) hurt
13. Carpenter is to house as poet is to verse. — (verse) novel writing
14. Lamp is to light as clock is to time. — (time) hands numbers
15. Palm is to hand as sole is to foot. — wrist finger (palm)

Copyright © 1991 American Education Publishing Co.

19

Reading Name:

More Analogies

Directions: Fill in the blanks with words of your own to complete each analogy. One is done for you.

1. Fuse is to firecracker as wick is to candle.
2. Wheel is to steering as brake is to stopping.
3. Scissors are to cut as needle is to sew.
4. Water is to skiing as rink is to skating.
5. Steam shovel is to dig as tractor is to plow.
6. Puck is to hockey as ball is to baseball.
7. Watch is to television as listen is to radio.
8. Geese is to goose as children is to child.
9. Multiply is to multiplication as subtract is to subtraction.
10. Milk is to cow as egg is to chicken.
11. Yellow is to banana as red is to tomato.
12. Fast is to slow as day is to night.
13. Pine is to tree as (varies) is to flower.
14. Zipper is to jacket as button is to shirt.
15. Museum is to painting as library is to book.
16. Petal is to flower as branch is to tree.
17. Cow is to barn as (varies) is to (varies).
18. (varies) is to bedroom as (varies) is to kitchen.
19. Teacher is to student as doctor is to patient.
20. Ice is to cold as (varies) is to (varies).

Copyright © 1991 American Education Publishing Co.

20

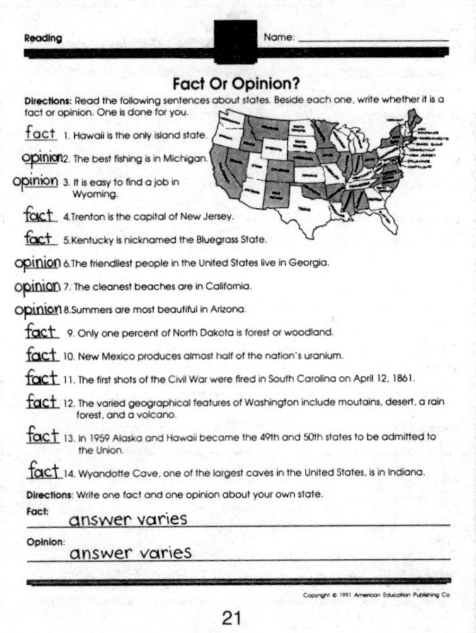
Reading Name:

Fact Or Opinion?

Directions: Read the following sentences about states. Beside each one, write whether it is a fact or opinion. One is done for you.

fact 1. Hawaii is the only island state.
opinion 2. The best fishing is in Michigan.
opinion 3. It is easy to find a job in Wyoming.
fact 4. Trenton is the capital of New Jersey.
fact 5. Kentucky is nicknamed the Bluegrass State.
opinion 6. The friendliest people in the United States live in Georgia.
opinion 7. The cleanest beaches are in California.
opinion 8. Summers are most beautiful in Arizona.
fact 9. Only one percent of North Dakota is forest or woodland.
fact 10. New Mexico produces almost half of the nation's uranium.
fact 11. The first shots of the Civil War were fired in South Carolina on April 12, 1861.
fact 12. The varied geographical features of Washington include moutains, desert, a rain forest, and a volcano.
fact 13. In 1959 Alaska and Hawaii became the 49th and 50th states to be admitted to the Union.
fact 14. Wyandotte Cave, one of the largest caves in the United States, is in Indiana.

Directions: Write one fact and one opinion about your own state.

Fact: answer varies

Opinion: answer varies

Copyright © 1991 American Education Publishing Co.

21

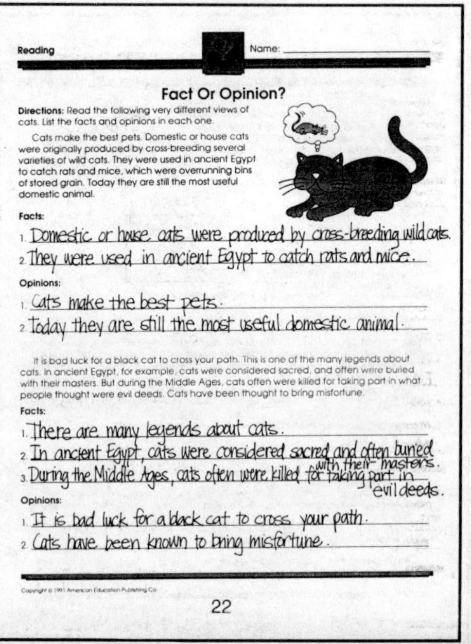
Reading Name:

Fact Or Opinion?

Directions: Read the following very different views of cats. List the facts and opinions in each one.

Cats make the best pets. Domestic or house cats were originally produced by cross-breeding several varieties of wild cats. They were used in ancient Egypt to catch rats and mice, which were overrunning bins of stored grain. Today they are still the most useful domestic animal.

Facts:
1. Domestic or house cats were produced by cross-breeding wild cats.
2. They were used in ancient Egypt to catch rats and mice.

Opinions:
1. Cats make the best pets.
2. Today they are still the most useful domestic animal.

It is bad luck for a black cat to cross your path. This is one of the many legends about cats. In ancient Egypt, for example, cats were considered sacred, and often were buried with their masters. But during the Middle Ages, cats often were killed for taking part in what people thought were evil deeds. Cats have been thought to bring misfortune.

Facts:
1. There are many legends about cats.
2. In ancient Egypt, cats were considered sacred and often buried with their masters.
3. During the Middle Ages, cats often were killed for taking part in evil deeds.

Opinions:
1. It is bad luck for a black cat to cross your path.
2. Cats have been known to bring misfortune.

Copyright © 1991 American Education Publishing Co.

22

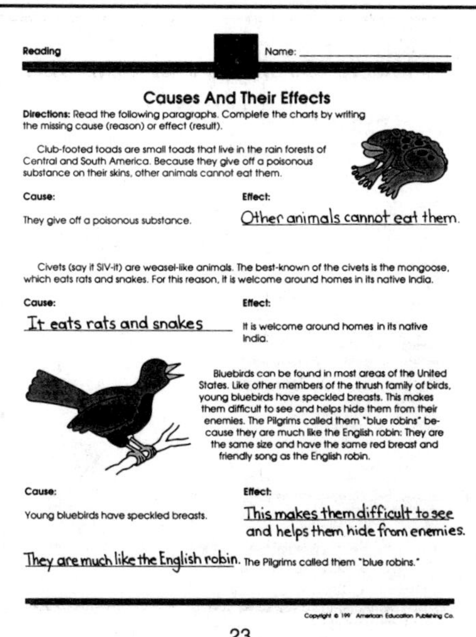

Reading Name: ____________

Causes And Their Effects

Directions: Read the following paragraphs. Complete the charts by writing the missing cause (reason) or effect (result).

Club-footed toads are small toads that live in the rain forests of Central and South America. Because they give off a poisonous substance on their skins, other animals cannot eat them.

Cause:	Effect:
They give off a poisonous substance.	Other animals cannot eat them.

Civets (say it SIV-it) are weasel-like animals. The best-known of the civets is the mongoose, which eats rats and snakes. For this reason, it is welcome around homes in its native India.

Cause:	Effect:
It eats rats and snakes	It is welcome around homes in its native India.

Bluebirds can be found in most areas of the United States. Like other members of the thrush family of birds, young bluebirds have speckled breasts. This makes them difficult to see and helps hide them from their enemies. The Pilgrims called them "blue robins" because they are much like the English robin: They are the same size and have the same red breast and friendly song as the English robin.

Cause:	Effect:
Young bluebirds have speckled breasts.	This makes them difficult to see and helps them hide from enemies.
They are much like the English robin.	The Pilgrims called them "blue robins."

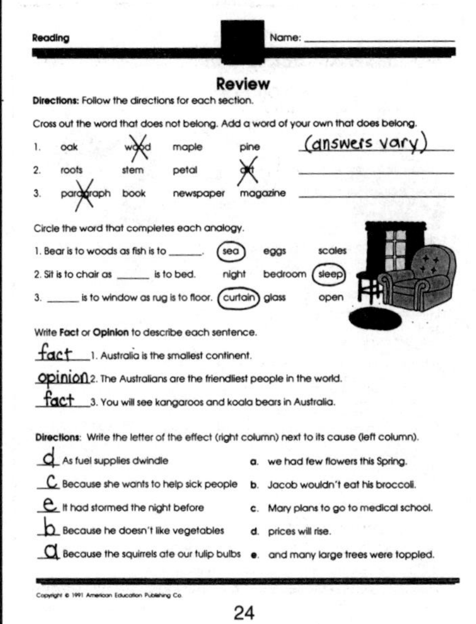

Reading Name: ____________

Review

Directions: Follow the directions for each section.

Cross out the word that does not belong. Add a word of your own that does belong.

1. oak ~~wood~~ maple pine (answers vary)
2. roots stem petal ~~oil~~
3. ~~paragraph~~ book newspaper magazine

Circle the word that completes each analogy.

1. Bear is to woods as fish is to ______. (sea) eggs scales
2. Sit is to chair as ______ is to bed. night bedroom (sleep)
3. ______ is to window as rug is to floor. (curtain) glass open

Write **Fact** or **Opinion** to describe each sentence.

fact 1. Australia is the smallest continent.
opinion 2. The Australians are the friendliest people in the world.
fact 3. You will see kangaroos and koala bears in Australia.

Directions: Write the letter of the effect (right column) next to its cause (left column).

d As fuel supplies dwindle — a. we had few flowers this Spring.
c Because she wants to help sick people — b. Jacob wouldn't eat his broccoli.
e It had stormed the night before — c. Mary plans to go to medical school.
b Because he doesn't like vegetables — d. prices will rise.
a Because the squirrels ate our tulip bulbs — e. and many large trees were toppled.

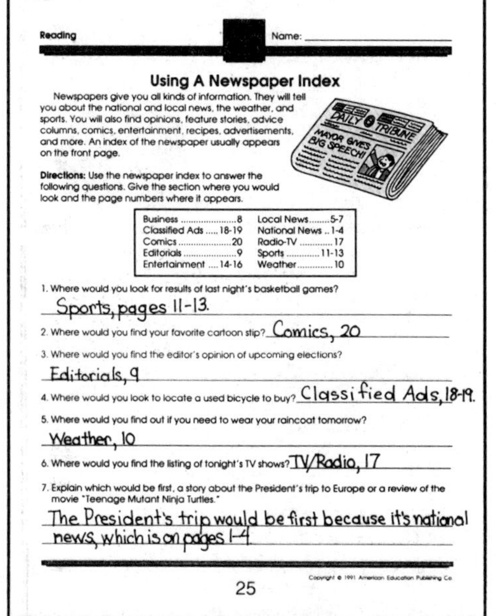

Reading Name: ____________

Using A Newspaper Index

Newspapers give you all kinds of information. They will tell you about the national and local news, the weather, and sports. You will also find opinions, feature stories, advice columns, comics, entertainment, recipes, advertisements, and more. An index of the newspaper usually appears on the front page.

Directions: Use the newspaper index to answer the following questions. Give the section where you would look and the page numbers where it appears.

1. Where would you look for results of last night's basketball games? Sports, pages 11-13.
2. Where would you find your favorite cartoon strip? Comics, 20
3. Where would you find the editor's opinion of upcoming elections? Editorials, 9
4. Where would you look to locate a used bicycle to buy? Classified Ads, 18-19.
5. Where would you find out if you need to wear your raincoat tomorrow? Weather, 10
6. Where would you find the listing of tonight's TV shows? TV/Radio, 17
7. Explain which would be first, a story about the President's trip to Europe or a review of the movie "Teenage Mutant Ninja Turtles." The President's trip would be first because it's national news, which is on pages 1-4

Reading Name: ____________

Reading A Map

Directions: Use the map of Columbus, Ohio, to answer the questions.

1. Does Highway 104 run east and west or north and south? east and west
2. What is the name of the freeway numbered 315? Olentangy Freeway
3. Which is further south, Bexley or Whitehall? Whitehall
4. What two freeways intersect (or cross) near the Port Columbus International Airport? 670 and 270
5. Which two cities are farther apart, Dublin and Upper Arlington or Dublin and Worthington? Dublin and Upper Arlington
6. In which direction would you be traveling if you drove from Grove City to Worthington? north

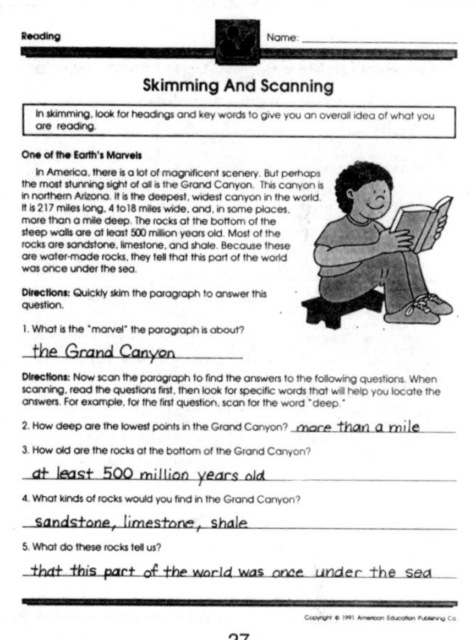

Reading Name: ____________

Skimming And Scanning

In skimming, look for headings and key words to give you an overall idea of what you are reading.

One of the Earth's Marvels

In America, there is a lot of magnificent scenery. But perhaps the most stunning sight of all is the Grand Canyon. This canyon is in northern Arizona. It is the deepest, widest canyon in the world. It is 217 miles long, 4 to18 miles wide, and, in some places, more than a mile deep. The rocks at the bottom of the steep walls are at least 500 million years old. Most of the rocks are sandstone, limestone, and shale. Because these are water-made rocks, they tell that this part of the world was once under the sea.

Directions: Quickly skim the paragraph to answer this question.

1. What is the "marvel" the paragraph is about? the Grand Canyon

Directions: Now scan the paragraph to find the answers to the following questions. When scanning, read the questions first, then look for specific words that will help you locate the answers. For example, for the first question, scan for the word "deep."

2. How deep are the lowest points in the Grand Canyon? more than a mile
3. How old are the rocks at the bottom of the Grand Canyon? at least 500 million years old
4. What kinds of rocks would you find in the Grand Canyon? sandstone, limestone, shale
5. What do these rocks tell us? that this part of the world was once under the sea

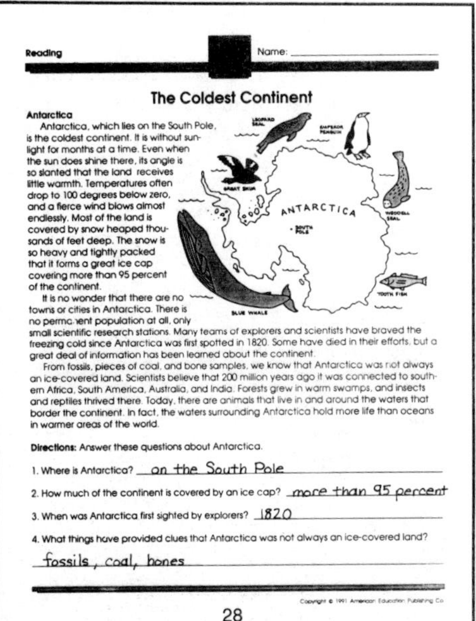

Reading Name: ____________

The Coldest Continent

Antarctica

Antarctica, which lies on the South Pole, is the coldest continent. It is without sunlight for months at a time. Even when the sun does shine there, its angle is so slanted that the land receives little warmth. Temperatures often drop to 100 degrees below zero, and a fierce wind blows almost endlessly. Most of the land is covered by snow heaped thousands of feet deep. The snow is so heavy and tightly packed that it forms a great ice cap covering more than 95 percent of the continent.

It is no wonder that there are no towns or cities in Antarctica. There is no permanent population at all, only small scientific research stations. Many teams of explorers and scientists have braved the freezing cold since Antarctica was first spotted in 1820. Some have died in their efforts, but a great deal of information has been learned about the continent.

From fossils, pieces of coal, and bone samples, we know that Antarctica was not always an ice-covered land. Scientists believe that 200 million years ago it was connected to southern Africa, South America, Australia, and India. Forests grew in warm swamps, and insects and reptiles thrived there. Today, there are animals that live in and around the waters that border the continent. In fact, the waters surrounding Antarctica hold more life than oceans in warmer areas of the world.

Directions: Answer these questions about Antarctica.

1. Where is Antarctica? on the South Pole
2. How much of the continent is covered by an ice cap? more than 95 percent
3. When was Antarctica first sighted by explorers? 1820
4. What things have provided clues that Antarctica was not always an ice-covered land? fossils, coal, bones

Name: ____________

The Other Pole

The Arctic Circle

On the other side of the world from Antarctica, at the northernmost part of the world, is another icy land. This is the Arctic Circle. It includes the North Pole itself, the northern fringes of three continents — Europe, Asia, and North America (including the state of Alaska) — as well as Greenland and other islands.

The seasons are opposite on the two ends of the world. When it is summer in Antarctica, it is winter in the Arctic Circle. In both places, there are very long periods of sunlight in summer and very long nights in the winter. On the poles themselves, there are six full months of sunlight and six full months of darkness each year.

Compared to Antarctica, the summers are surprisingly mild in some areas of the Arctic Circle. Much of the snow cover may melt, and temperatures often reach 50 degrees in July. But neither of the polar regions can support plant life. Antarctica is covered by water — frozen water, of course — so nothing can grow there. Plant growth is limited in the polar regions not only by the cold, but also by wind, lack of water, and the long winter darkness.

In the Far North, willow trees do grow, but only to be a few inches high! The annual rings — the circles within the trunk of a tree that show its age and how fast it grows — in these trees are so narrow that you need a microscope to see them.

A permanently frozen layer of soil, called "permafrost," keeps roots from growing deep enough into the ground to anchor a plant. Even if a plant could survive the cold temperatures, it could not grow roots deep enough or strong enough to allow the plant to get very big.

Directions: Answer these questions about the Arctic Circle.

1. What three continents have land included in the Arctic Circle?

a. Europe b. Asia c. North America

2. Is the Arctic Circle generally warmer or colder than Antarctica? warmer

3. What are the annual rings of a tree? the circles in the trunk of the tree that tell how old it is and how fast it is growing

4. What is "permafrost"? a permanently frozen layer of soil

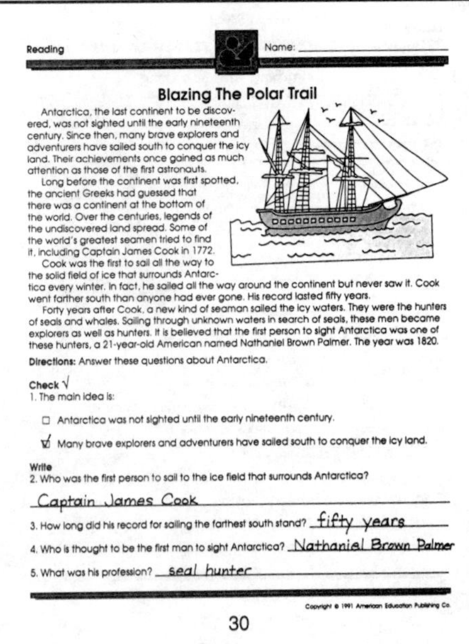

Name: ____________

Blazing The Polar Trail

Antarctica, the last continent to be discovered, was not sighted until the early nineteenth century. Since then, many brave explorers and adventurers have sailed south to conquer the icy land. Their achievements once gained as much attention as those of the first astronauts.

Long before the continent was first spotted, the ancient Greeks had guessed that there was a continent at the bottom of the world. Over the centuries, legends of the undiscovered land spread. Some of the world's greatest seamen tried to find it, including Captain James Cook in 1772.

Cook was the first to sail all the way to the solid field of ice that surrounds Antarctica every winter. In fact, he sailed all the way around the continent but never saw it. Cook went farther south than anyone had ever gone. His record lasted fifty years.

Forty years after Cook, a new kind of seaman sailed the icy waters. They were the hunters of seals and whales. Sailing through unknown waters in search of seals, these men became explorers as well as hunters. It is believed that the first person to sight Antarctica was one of these hunters, a 21-year-old American named Nathaniel Brown Palmer. The year was 1820.

Directions: Answer these questions about Antarctica.

Check √

1. The main idea is:

- ☐ Antarctica was not sighted until the early nineteenth century.
- ☑ Many brave explorers and adventurers have sailed south to conquer the icy land.

Write

2. Who was the first person to sail to the ice field that surrounds Antarctica?

Captain James Cook

3. How long did his record for sailing the farthest south stand? fifty years

4. Who is thought to be the first man to sight Antarctica? Nathaniel Brown Palmer

5. What was his profession? seal hunter

Name: ____________

Seals

Seals are **aquatic** mammals that have kept a liking for land. Some seals stay in the sea for weeks or months at a time, even sleeping in the water. But all seals need the land at some time. To avoid people and other animals, they pick **secluded** spots to come onto the land.

The 31 different kinds of seals belong to a group of animals that is often called "pinnipeds," or fin-footed. Their fins, or flippers, make them very good swimmers and divers. Their nostrils close tightly when they dive. They have been know to stay **submerged** for as long as a half-hour at a time!

Seals are warm-blooded animals that can adjust to various temperatures. They live in both **temperate** and cold climates. Besides their fur, seals have a thick layer of fat called "blubber" to help protect them against the cold. It is harder for seals to cool themselves in hot weather than to warm themselves in cold weather. They sometimes can become so overheated that they die.

Directions: Answer these questions about seals.

Check √

1. Based on the other words in the sentence, what is the correct definition for "aquatic"?
   - ☐ living on the land
   - ☑ living on or in the sea
   - ☐ living in large groups
2. Based on the other words in the sentence, what is the correct definition for "secluded"?
   - ☐ rocky
   - ☑ private or hidden
   - ☐ near other animals
3. Based on the other words in the sentence, what is the correct definition for "submerged"?
   - ☑ under the water
   - ☐ on top of the water
   - ☐ in groups
4. Based on the other word in the sentence, what is the correct definition for "temperate"?
   - ☐ rainy
   - ☐ measured on a thermometer
   - ☑ warm

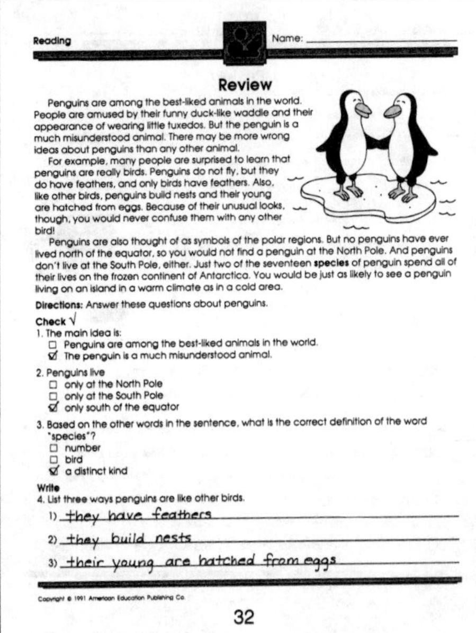

Name: ____________

Review

Penguins are among the best-liked animals in the world. People are amused by their funny duck-like waddle and their appearance of wearing little tuxedos. But the penguin is a much misunderstood animal. There may be more wrong ideas about penguins than any other animal.

For example, many people are surprised to learn that penguins are really birds. Penguins do not fly, but they do have feathers, and only birds have feathers. Also, like other birds, penguins build nests and their young are hatched from eggs. Because of their unusual looks, though, you would never confuse them with any other bird!

Penguins are also thought of as symbols of the polar regions. But no penguins have ever lived north of the equator, so you would not find a penguin at the North Pole. And penguins don't live at the South Pole, either. Just two of the seventeen **species** of penguin spend all of their lives on the frozen continent of Antarctica. You would be just as likely to see a penguin living on an island in a warm climate as in a cold area.

Directions: Answer these questions about penguins.

Check √

1. The main idea is:
   - ☐ Penguins are among the best-liked animals in the world.
   - ☑ The penguin is a much misunderstood animal.
2. Penguins live
   - ☐ only at the North Pole
   - ☐ only at the South Pole
   - ☑ only south of the equator
3. Based on the other words in the sentence, what is the correct definition of the word "species"?
   - ☐ number
   - ☐ bird
   - ☑ a distinct kind

Write

4. List three ways penguins are like other birds.

1) they have feathers
2) they build nests
3) their young are hatched from eggs

Notes

Notes

Name: ____________________

What Are They?

Directions: Read each group of words. Cross out the word that does not belong. Then add a word of your own that does belong. One is done for you.

1. wren	robin	~~feather~~	sparrow	eagle	bluebird
2. sofa	stool	chair	carpet	bench	______
3. lettuce	salad	corn	broccoli	spinach	______
4. pencil	chalk	crayon	pen	drawing	______
5. perch	shark	penguin	bass	tuna	______
6. rapid	quick	unhurried	swift	speedy	______
7. lemon	daisy	melon	lime	grapefruit	______

Directions: Above each group of words, write a category name from the word box. Then write a word of your own that belongs in each group.

parts of the leg
winter sports
storms
parts of a radio

______
blizzard
hurricane
thunder
______

______
ankle
shin
thigh
______

______
antenna
speaker
battery
______

______
hockey
ice skating
bobsledding
______

Name: ______________________

Today's Regional Forecast

The very warm early-spring weather will continue to spread along the East Coast today. With some sunshine, afternoon temperatures will climb to 90 degrees in spots. Columbia, S.C., and neighboring areas could reach 100 degrees. Showers are expected from Washington, D.C., to New York City. Severe thunderstorms are likely in Virginia and North Carolina. Central South Carolina will be under a tornado watch during the afternoon.

Directions: Find words in the above forecast that belong in the categories below. Write them in the correct lists.

Cities

1. ______________________
2. ______________________
3. ______________________

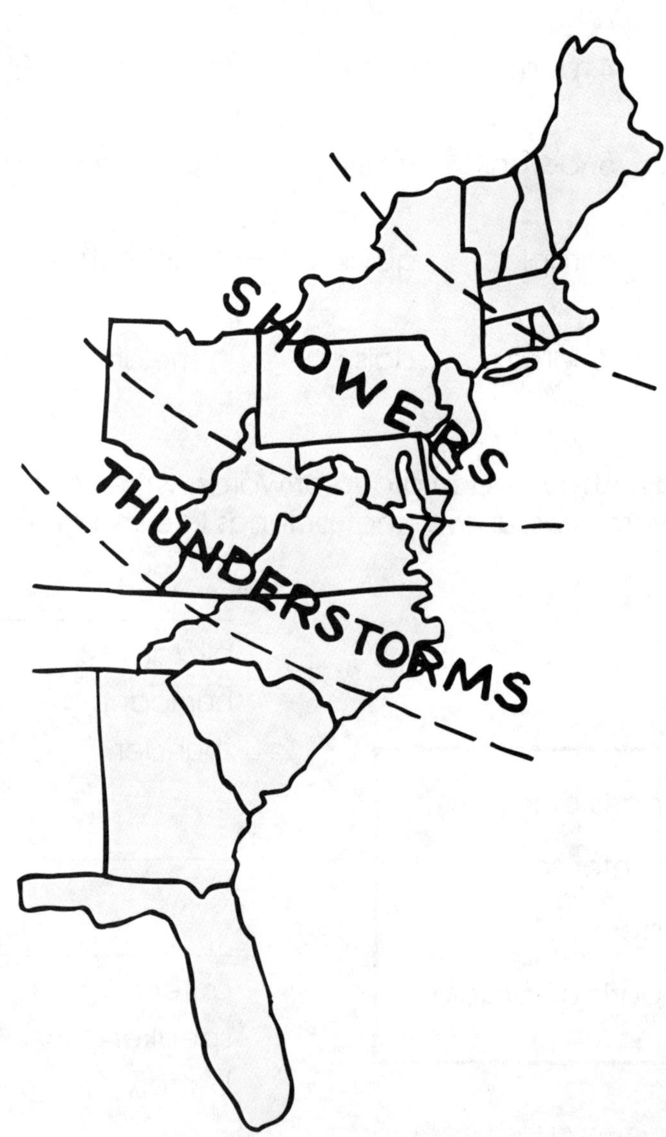

States

1. ______________________
2. ______________________
3. ______________________

Weather Conditions

1. ______________________
2. ______________________
3. ______________________
4. ______________________

Name: ______________________

How Do They Relate

Directions: Circle the correct word to fill in the missing part of each analogy. One is done for you.

1. Scissors are to paper as saw is to wood.	fold	(scissors)	thin
2. Man is to boy as woman is to ______________.	mother	girl	lady
3. ______________ is to cellar as sky is to ground.	down	attic	up
4. Rag is to dust as ______________ is to sweep.	floor	straw	broom
5. Freezer is to cold as stove is to ______________.	cook	hot	recipe
6. Car is to ______________ as book is to bookshelf.	ride	gas	garage
7. Window is to ______________ as car is to metal.	glass	clear	house
8. Eyes are to seeing as feet are to ______________.	legs	walking	shoes
9. Gasoline is to car as ______________ is to lamp.	electricity	plug	cord
10. Refrigerator is to food as ______________ is to clothes.	fold	material	closet
11. Floor is to down as ceiling is to ______________.	high	over	up
12. Pillow is to soft as rock is to ______________.	dirt	hard	hurt
13. Carpenter is to house as poet is to ______________.	verse	novel	writing
14. Lamp is to light as clock is to ______________.	time	hands	numbers
15. ______________ is to hand as sole is to foot.	wrist	finger	palm

Name: ______________________

More Analogies

Directions: Fill in the blanks with words of your own to complete each analogy. One is done for you.

1. Fuse is to firecracker as wick is to candle.
2. Wheel is to steering as ________________ is to stopping.
3. Scissors are to ________________ as needle is to sew.
4. Water is to skiing as rink is to ________________.
5. Steam shovel is to dig as tractor is to ________________.
6. Puck is to hockey as ________________ is to baseball.
7. Watch is to television as ________________ is to radio.
8. ________________ is to goose as children is to child.
9. Multiply is to multiplication as ________________ is to subtraction.
10. Milk is to ________________ as egg is to ________________.
11. Yellow is to banana as ________________ is to tomato.
12. ________________ is to slow as day is to night.
13. Pine is to tree as ________________ is to flower.
14. Zipper is to jacket as ________________ is to shirt.
15. Museum is to painting as library is to ________________.
16. Petal is to ________________ as branch is to ________________.
17. Cow is to barn as ________________ is to ________________.
18. ________________ is to bedroom as ________________ is to kitchen.
19. Teacher is to ________________ as ________________ is to patient.
20. Ice is to cold as ________________ is to ________________.

Name: ______________________

Fact Or Opinion?

Directions: Read the following sentences about states. Beside each one, write whether it is a fact or opinion. One is done for you.

fact 1. Hawaii is the only island state.

_______ 2. The best fishing is in Michigan.

_______ 3. It is easy to find a job in Wyoming.

_______ 4.Trenton is the capital of New Jersey.

_______ 5.Kentucky is nicknamed the Bluegrass State.

_______ 6.The friendliest people in the United States live in Georgia.

_______ 7. The cleanest beaches are in California.

_______ 8. Summers are most beautiful in Arizona.

_______ 9. Only one percent of North Dakota is forest or woodland.

_______ 10. New Mexico produces almost half of the nation's uranium.

_______ 11. The first shots of the Civil War were fired in South Carolina on April 12, 1861.

_______ 12. The varied geographical features of Washington include moutains, desert, a rain forest, and a volcano.

_______ 13. In 1959, Alaska and Hawaii became the 49th and 50th states to be admitted to the Union.

_______ 14. Wyandotte Cave, one of the largest caves in the United States, is in Indiana.

Directions: Write one fact and one opinion about your own state.

Fact:

____

Opinion:

____

Name: ____________________

Fact Or Opinion?

Directions: Read the following very different views of cats. List the facts and opinions in each one.

Cats make the best pets. Domestic or house cats were originally produced by cross-breeding several varieties of wild cats. They were used in ancient Egypt to catch rats and mice, which were overrunning bins of stored grain. Today they are still the most useful domestic animal.

Facts:

1. ____________________

2. ____________________

Opinions:

1. ____________________

2. ____________________

It is bad luck for a black cat to cross your path. This is one of the many legends about cats. In ancient Egypt, for example, cats were considered sacred, and often were buried with their masters. But during the Middle Ages, cats often were killed for taking part in what people thought were evil deeds. Cats have been thought to bring misfortune.

Facts:

1. ____________________

2. ____________________

3. ____________________

Opinions:

1. ____________________

2. ____________________

Name: ______________________

Causes And Their Effects

Directions: Read the following paragraphs. Complete the charts by writing the missing cause (reason) or effect (result).

Club-footed toads are small toads that live in the rain forests of Central and South America. Because they give off a poisonous substance on their skins, other animals cannot eat them.

Cause:	**Effect:**
They give off a poisonous substance.	______________________

Civets (say it SIV-it) are weasel-like animals. The best-known of the civets is the mongoose, which eats rats and snakes. For this reason, it is welcome around homes in its native India.

Cause:	**Effect:**
______________________	It is welcome around homes in its native India.

Bluebirds can be found in most areas of the United States. Like other members of the thrush family of birds, young bluebirds have speckled breasts. This makes them difficult to see and helps hide them from their enemies. The Pilgrims called them "blue robins" because they are much like the English robin: They are the same size and have the same red breast and friendly song as the English robin.

Cause:	**Effect:**
Young bluebirds have speckled breasts.	______________________
______________________	The Pilgrims called them "blue robins."

Name: ______________________

Review

Directions: Follow the directions for each section.

Cross out the word that does not belong. Add a word of your own that does belong.

1.	oak	wood	maple	pine	______________
2.	roots	stem	petal	dirt	______________
3.	paragraph	book	newspaper	magazine	______________

Circle the word that completes each analogy.

1. Bear is to woods as fish is to ______.	sea	eggs	scales
2. Sit is to chair as ______ is to bed.	night	bedroom	sleep
3. ______ is to window as rug is to floor.	curtain	glass	open

Write **Fact** or **Opinion** to describe each sentence.

__________ 1. Australia is the smallest continent.

__________ 2. The Australians are the friendliest people in the world.

__________ 3. You will see kangaroos and koala bears in Australia.

Directions: Write the letter of the effect (right column) next to its cause (left column).

_____ As fuel supplies dwindle	**a.** we had few flowers this spring.
_____ Because she wants to help sick people	**b.** Jacob wouldn't eat his broccoli.
_____ It had stormed the night before	**c.** Mary plans to go to medical school.
_____ Because he doesn't like vegetables	**d.** prices will rise.
_____ Because the squirrels ate our tulip bulbs	**e.** and many large trees were toppled.

Name: ____________________

Using A Newspaper Index

Newspapers give you all kinds of information. They will tell you about the national and local news, the weather, and sports. You will also find opinions, feature stories, advice columns, comics, entertainment, recipes, advertisements, and more. An index of the newspaper usually appears on the front page.

Directions: Use the newspaper index to answer the following questions..Give the section where you would look and the page numbers where it appears.

Business	8	Local News	5-7
Classified Ads	18-19	National News	1-4
Comics	20	Radio-TV	17
Editorials	9	Sports	11-13
Entertainment	14-16	Weather	10

1. Where would you look for results of last night's basketball games?

____

2. Where would you find your favorite cartoon stip?______________________________

3. Where would you find the editor's opinion of upcoming elections?

____

4. Where would you look to locate a used bicycle to buy?______________________________

5. Where would you find out if you need to wear your raincoat tomorrow?

____

6. Where would you find the listing of tonight's TV shows?______________________________

7. Explain which would be first, a story about the President's trip to Europe or a review of the movie "Teenage Mutant Ninja Turtles".

____

____

Name: ______________________

Practical Reading Skills: Map

Directions: Use the map of Columbus, Ohio, to answer the questions.

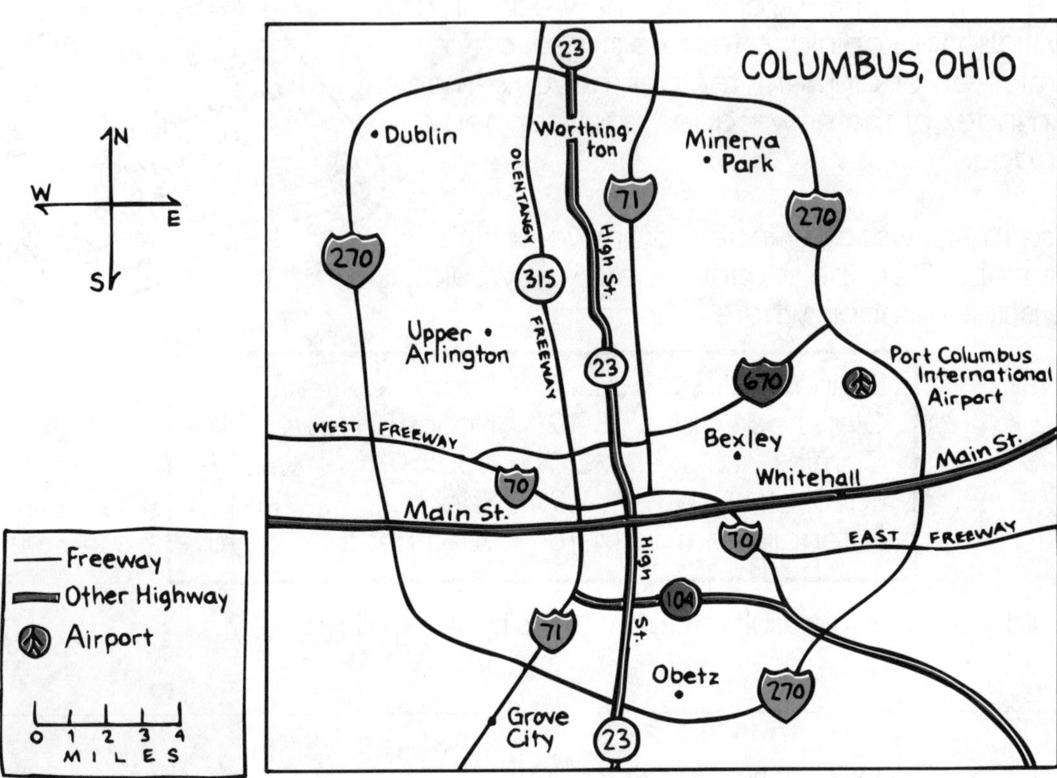

1. Does Highway 104 run east and west or north and south? ______________________

2. What is the name of the freeway numbered 315? ______________________

3. Which is further south, Bexley or Whitehall? ______________________

4. What two freeways intersect (or cross) near the Port Columbus International Airport?

____

5. Which two cities are farther apart, Dublin and Upper Arlington or Dublin and Worthington?

____

6. In which direction would you be traveling if you drove from Grove City to Worthington?

____

Name: ____________________

Skimming/Scanning

In skimming, look for headings and key words to give you an overall idea of what you are reading.

One of the Earth's Marvels

In America, there is a lot of magnificent scenery. But perhaps the most stunning sight of all is the Grand Canyon. This canyon is in northern Arizona. It is the deepest, widest canyon in the world. It is 217 miles long, 4 to18 miles wide, and, in some places, more than a mile deep. The rocks at the bottom of the steep walls are at least 500 million years old. Most of the rocks are sandstone, limestone, and shale. Because these are water-made rocks, they tell that this part of the world was once under the sea.

Directions: Quickly skim the paragraph to answer this question.

1. What is the "marvel" the paragraph is about?

____

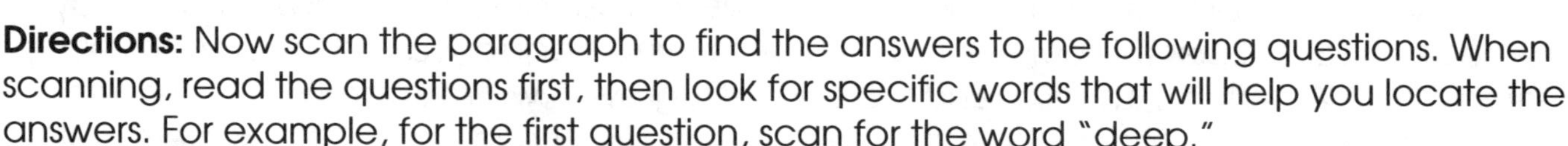

Directions: Now scan the paragraph to find the answers to the following questions. When scanning, read the questions first, then look for specific words that will help you locate the answers. For example, for the first question, scan for the word "deep."

2. How deep are the lowest points in the Grand Canyon? ____________________

3. How old are the rocks at the bottom of the Grand Canyon?

____

4. What kinds of rocks would you find in the Grand Canyon?

____

5. What do these rocks tell us?

____

Reading

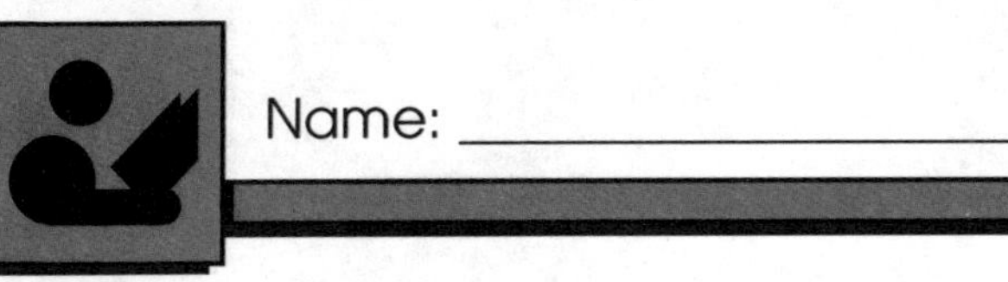

Name: ____________________

The Coldest Continent

Antarctica

Antarctica, which lies on the South Pole, is the coldest continent. It is without sunlight for months at a time. Even when the sun does shine there, its angle is so slanted that the land receives little warmth. Temperatures often drop to 100 degrees below zero, and a fierce wind blows almost endlessly. Most of the land is covered by snow heaped thousands of feet deep. The snow is so heavy and tightly packed that it forms a great ice cap covering more than 95 percent of the continent.

It is no wonder that there are no towns or cities in Antarctica. There is no permanent population at all, only small scientific research stations. Many teams of explorers and scientists have braved the freezing cold since Antarctica was first spotted in 1820. Some have died in their efforts, but a great deal of information has been learned about the continent.

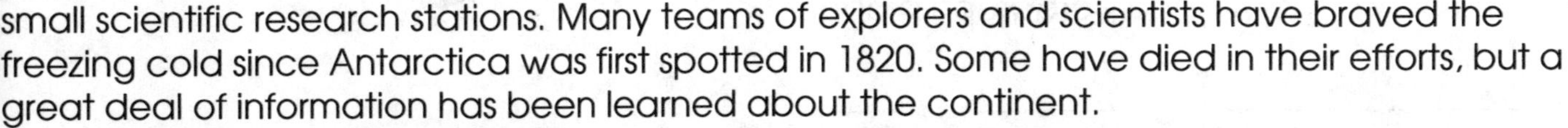

From fossils, pieces of coal, and bone samples, we know that Antarctica was not always an ice-covered land. Scientists believe that 200 million years ago it was connected to southern Africa, South America, Australia, and India. Forests grew in warm swamps, and insects and reptiles thrived there. Today, there are animals that live in and around the waters that border the continent. In fact, the waters surrounding Antarctica hold more life than oceans in warmer areas of the world.

Directions: Answer these questions about Antarctica.

1. Where is Antarctica? ____________________

2. How much of the continent is covered by an ice cap? ____________________

3. When was Antarctica first sighted by explorers? ____________________

4. What things have provided clues that Antarctica was not always an ice-covered land?

____

Name: ____________________

Remembering What You Read: The Other Pole

The Arctic Circle

On the other side of the world from Antarctica, at the northernmost part of the world, is another icy land. This is the Arctic Circle. It includes the North Pole itself, the northern fringes of three continents — Europe, Asia, and North America (including the state of Alaska) — as well as Greenland and other islands.

The seasons are opposite on the two ends of the world. When it is summer in Antarctica, it is winter in the Arctic Circle. In both places, there are very long periods of sunlight in summer and very long nights in the winter. On the poles themselves, there are six full months of sunlight and six full months of darkness each year.

Compared to Antarctica, the summers are surprisingly mild in some areas of the Arctic Circle. Much of the snow cover may melt, and temperatures often reach 50 degrees in July. But neither of the polar regions can support plant life. Antarctica is covered by water — frozen water, of course — so nothing can grow there. Plant growth is limited in the polar regions not only by the cold, but also by wind, lack of water, and the long winter darkness.

In the Far North, willow trees do grow, but only to be a few inches high! The annual rings — the circles within the trunk of a tree that show its age and how fast it grows — in these trees are so narrow that you need a microscope to see them.

A permanently frozen layer of soil, called "permafrost," keeps roots from growing deep enough into the ground to anchor a plant. Even if a plant could survive the cold temperatures, it could not grow roots deep enough or strong enough to allow the plant to get very big.

Directions: Answer these questions about the Arctic Circle.

1. What three continents have land included in the Arctic Circle?

a.____________________ b.____________________ c.____________________

2. Is the Arctic Circle generally warmer or colder than Antarctica?____________________

3. What are the annual rings of a tree? ____________________

4. What is "permafrost"? ____________________

Name: ____________________

Main Idea: Blazing The Polar Trail

Antarctica, the last continent to be discovered, was not sighted until the early nineteenth century. Since then, many brave explorers and adventurers have sailed south to conquer the icy land. Their achievements once gained as much attention as those of the first astronauts.

Long before the continent was first spotted, the ancient Greeks had guessed that there was a continent at the bottom of the world. Over the centuries, legends of the undiscovered land spread. Some of the world's greatest seamen tried to find it, including Captain James Cook in 1772.

Cook was the first to sail all the way to the solid field of ice that surrounds Antarctica every winter. In fact, he sailed all the way around the continent but never saw it. Cook went farther south than anyone had ever gone. His record lasted fifty years.

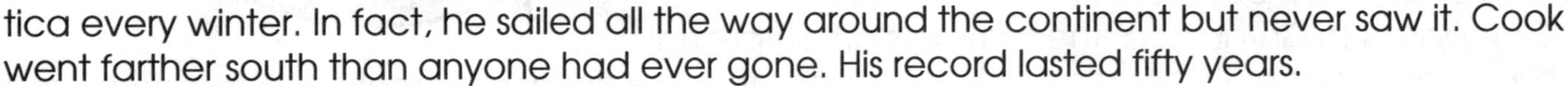

Forty years after Cook, a new kind of seaman sailed the icy waters. They were the hunters of seals and whales. Sailing through unknown waters in search of seals, these men became explorers as well as hunters. It is believed that the first person to sight Antarctica was one of these hunters, a 21-year-old American named Nathaniel Brown Palmer. The year was 1820.

Directions: Answer these questions about Antarctica.

Check √

1. The main idea is:

☐ Antarctica was not sighted until the early nineteenth century.

☐ Many brave explorers and adventurers have sailed south to conquer the icy land.

Write

2. Who was the first person to sail to the ice field that surrounds Antarctica?

____

3. How long did his record for sailing the farthest south stand? ____________________

4. Who is thought to be the first man to sight Antarctica? ____________________

5. What was his profession? ____________________

Name: ____________________

Context: Seals

Seals are **aquatic** mammals that have kept a liking for land. Some seals stay in the sea for weeks or months at a time, even sleeping in the water. But all seals need the land at some time. To avoid people and other animals, they pick **secluded** spots to come onto the land.

The 31 different kinds of seals belong to a group of animals that is often called "pinnipeds", or fin-footed. Their fins, or flippers, make them very good swimmers and divers. Their nostrils close tightly when they dive. They have been known to stay **submerged** for as long as a half-hour at a time!

Seals are warm-blooded animals that can adjust to various temperatures. They live in both **temperate** and cold climates. Besides their fur, seals have a thick layer of fat called "blubber" to help protect them against the cold. It is harder for seals to cool themselves in hot weather than to warm themselves in cold weather. They sometimes can become so overheated that they die.

Directions: Answer these questions about seals.

Check √

1. Based on the other words in the sentence, what is the correct definition for "aquatic"?
   - ☐ living on the land
   - ☐ living on or in the sea
   - ☐ living in large groups

2. Based on the other words in the sentence, what is the correct definition for "secluded"?
   - ☐ rocky
   - ☐ private or hidden
   - ☐ near other animals

3. Based on the other words in the sentence, what is the correct definition for "submerged"?
   - ☐ under the water
   - ☐ on top of the water
   - ☐ in groups

4. Based on the other words in the sentence, what is the correct definition for "temperate"?
   - ☐ rainy
   - ☐ measured on a thermometer
   - ☐ warm

Name: ______________________

Review

Penguins are among the best-liked animals in the world. People are amused by their funny duck-like waddle and their appearance of wearing little tuxedos. But the penguin is a much misunderstood animal. There may be more wrong ideas about penguins than any other animal.

For example, many people are surprised to learn that penguins are really birds. Penguins do not fly, but they do have feathers, and only birds have feathers. Also, like other birds, penguins build nests and their young are hatched from eggs. Because of their unusual looks, though, you would never confuse them with any other bird!

Penguins are also thought of as symbols of the polar regions. But no penguins have ever lived north of the equator, so you would not find a penguin on the North Pole. Penguins don't live at the South Pole, either. Just two of the seventeen **species** of penguin spend all of their lives on the frozen continent of Antarctica. You would be just as likely to see a penguin living on an island in a warm climate as in a cold area.

Directions: Answer these questions about penguins.

Check √

1. The main idea is:
   - ☐ Penguins are among the best-liked animals in the world.
   - ☐ The penguin is a much misunderstood animal.

2. Penguins live
   - ☐ only at the North Pole
   - ☐ only at the South Pole
   - ☐ only south of the equator

3. Based on the other words in the sentence, what is the correct definition of the word "species"?
   - ☐ number
   - ☐ bird
   - ☐ a distinct kind

Write

4. List three ways penguins are like other birds.

   1) ____

   2) ____

   3) ____